PIONEER LIFE IN KENTUCKY

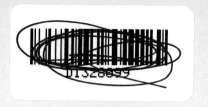

Daniel Drake, M.D.

(From Lith. by F. D'Avignon, from Daguerreotype by Ph. Haas, N. Y.)

Pioneer Life in Kentucky
1785-1800

BY

DANIEL DRAKE, M.D.

Edited, from the original manuscript,
with introductory comments and
a biographical sketch by

EMMET FIELD HORINE, M.D.

HENRY SCHUMAN · NEW YORK

PREFACE

T HIS book consists of a series of "reminiscential" letters written by Dr. Daniel Drake in response to the urgent requests of his children for a family record. No two letters are alike in style. To his youngest child, Harriet Echo, he seems to write with an especial tenderness. For a son-in-law, Alexander Hamilton McGuffey, he describes the cultivation and use of Indian corn, enlivening the letter with many allusions to authors and books. Letter VI is to an adopted daughter who is neurotic and he apparently subtly advises that she cultivate a taste for the quiet beauties of nature. As one reads these letters with care it seems possible to fathom the sentiment Drake entertained toward each person to whom he is writing.

The first edition of this book as arranged by his son, Charles Daniel Drake, was published in 1870 as Volume No. 6 of the Ohio Valley Historical Series (Robert Clarke & Co., Cincinnati, Ohio). The demand for this edition has made every copy a collector's item. Only one reprint was published (1907) but, in catalogues of Americana, this is even more rarely listed than the earlier edition. In view of its historical significance and rarity, it is surprising that another edition has not been issued before now.

This book, although written by the most eminent early nineteenth century physician of the Central West, is not a medical treatise. It is an intimate and detailed portrayal of farm and family life in a fascinating and significant period of the United States. It stands unique as an extraordinarily faithful account of the simple but varied pursuits of the pioneer. In this day of a world, divided and frustrated, vainly seeking to find security in collectivism and materialism, this book affords a wholesome contrast in its delineation of the accomplishments of individual effort and perseverance.

Anyone seriously interested in the history of the last decade of the eighteenth century in America must familiarize himself with this classic description of pioneer life. Only in recent years have historians generally come to recognize that the mere recording of the activities of rulers, of wars and of their consequences is a shallow and deplorably inadequate record of the past. *Almost a century ago* Daniel Drake, with astounding acumen, clearly expressed this modern concept:

The history of a nation is not to be read in the lives of its generals and politicians merely, but comprehends, as its necessary elements, the history of all *classes* of the people, and all *branches* of intellectual, moral, religious, and physical industry . . .[1]

Albert J. Beveridge in his *Abraham Lincoln* made use of and quotes from *Pioneer Life in Kentucky*. In addition,

[1] Daniel Drake: *Discourses Delivered by Appointment before the Cincinnati Medical Library Association, January 9th and 10th, 1852,* (Cincinnati: Moore & Anderson, 1852), page 35.

he gives a digest of three remarkable letters on slavery written by Dr. Drake which appeared in *The National Intelligencer* (Washington) in April 1851. These letters have since been published in book format.[2] Theodore Roosevelt was introduced to Drake's Kentucky pioneers by the late Col. Reuben T. Durrett (1824-1913) of Louisville, in whose library he gathered some basic materials for *The Winning of the West.* It was quite apparent that Roosevelt carefully followed the narrative of Drake's *Pioneer Life*, to which he refers as "an invaluable work." Almost two pages are quoted verbatim. We would agree with Mr. J. Christian Bay, Librarian Emeritus of the John Crerar Library, Chicago, when he refers to Drake's work as "the greatest of all Kentucky books."

Aside from its historical importance, *Pioneer Life in Kentucky* cannot fail to interest the physician, the psychologist, the clergyman, the botanist, the naturalist, the farmer and the housewife. Thoughtful young people as well as adults will find here fascinating reading. Dr. Drake's whimsical and quaint diction are delightful and refreshing. The "flavor" is on a par with the impression of absolute truthfulness which one obtains in reading these letters.

When Mr. Henry Schuman requested that I edit *Pioneer Life in Kentucky*, the 1870 edition was, quite logically, consulted. I was then under the impression that the letters comprising it had been published without essential changes. While carefully preparing the first two letters, I

[2] Daniel Drake: *Letters on Slavery . . . Reprinted from The National Intelligencer . . . With an Introduction by Emmet Field Horine*, (Schuman's, 1940).

was surprised to encounter several passages where the narrative seemed to waver. This was so unlike the diction of the many other writings of Dr. Daniel Drake with which I was more familiar that I became suspicious. Fortunately the original letters in manuscript are in the Library of the Cincinnati General Hospital. I was thus able to compare them with the text of the 1870 Edition. To my astonishment, I discovered that hundreds of changes had been made by the editor without notation. Dozens of important paragraphs had been deleted with no indication whatever of such emasculation. The manuscript of Letters I and II prepared from the 1870 Edition was discarded. Through the courtesy of Miss Eva G. Kyte, the efficient Medical Librarian and her able assistant, Miss Alice E. McCaffrey, of the Cincinnati General Hospital, I was able to make a photostat of the letters in their entirety. My sincere appreciation and thanks are tendered Miss Kyte and her assistant who thus made possible this Edition.

I have faithfully followed the manuscript throughout in its original form. Because of the flavor of Drake's diction I have made but few deletions of repetitious or slightly irrelevant material. Such omissions have been indicated by the customary marks. My own additions to the text invariably have been placed in brackets. Dr. Drake made liberal use of punctuation marks, especially the long (technically, the *em*) dash, many of which have been retained. However, some of his sentences which seemed too long have been shortened merely by the elimination of connectives. He often used the ampersand (&) as was the custom in his day.

Dr. Drake was usually a very good speller although, at

times, inconsistent. *Timid* may appear with either a single or double *m*. According to Dr. Drake, *ammunition* has one *m* which may be justified by its derivation from the French. The appeal of *turkies* is irresistible. These incorrect spellings have been preserved and are set in boldface type. His archaic and obsolete words also have been retained but without marks of identification. In respect to capitalization the manuscript has been followed. His frequent use of underlining is shown by italics.

Throughout the editing of this book from the original manuscript I have had at hand the 1870 version by Charles D. Drake. I must admit frequent irritation because of the many liberties taken with the manuscript. Charles' futile attempts to improve his father's diction are extremely exasperating and he exhibits an utter lack both of imagination and humor. When Dr. Drake writes in the third letter: "Its after 1 o'c'k: I'm in the Sabbath—so good night!"— Charles has deleted, *I'm in the Sabbath!*

These letters were written hurriedly without the slightest idea that they would ever be published, as will be clear even to the casual reader of them. Dr. Drake did not bother to consult source material and is, therefore, guilty of slight inaccuracies. No attempt has been made to correct all such lapses because the publisher and I agreed as to the wisdom of reducing to a minimum critical notes and corrections. However, reference to the footnotes is essential to a correct appraisal of the text. Only the more prominent persons have been identified.

There are many to whom I must tender my thanks for material assistance. Mrs. Daniel B. Ruggles (Alice McGuffey Morrill), great granddaughter of Dr. Drake loaned me portraits of Harriet Echo, Elizabeth, Charles Daniel and his wife, Margaret. Dr. Lawrence Reynolds, of Detroit, loaned the portrait of Dr. Drake which appears as the frontispiece. The Curator of The Filson Club, Louisville, Miss Ludie J. Kinkead, kindly criticized my handling of Letter I in addition to assisting with some of the references. Miss Dorcas Ruthenburg has listened to parts of the manuscript and given valuable advice. My son-in-law and daughter (Dorothy), Mr. and Mrs. Herbert E. Arntson, of Washington State College, have both been helpfully critical. Miss Edna J. Grauman and her assistants in the Reference Department and Miss Ellen T. Harding of the Kentucky Room of the Louisville Free Public Library have all shown willingness in answering my numerous questions. Miss Blake Beem of the Medical Library of the University of Louisville has shown interest at all times and has been more than willing to aid. Help, for which I am greatly indebted, was obtained from the staffs of many other libraries including The Library of Congress, the Historical and Philosophical Society of Ohio, the Cincinnati Public Library, The State Historical Society of Missouri, the Chattanooga Public Library, and the St. Louis Public Library. Miss Elizabeth Mitchell of Mayslick, Kentucky, a descendant of one of the pioneers, Mr. John Shotwell, has furnished important information. To Dr. Isaac Starr, Dean, and his Assistant, Dr. William B. Kennedy, of the School of Medicine, University of Pennsylvania, I wish to express appreciation for help in identifying some of their students. Mr. Henry Schuman has kept in

PREFACE

touch with the progress of the editing from the beginning
and my thanks are herewith tendered him for his valuable
advice and encouragement. Finally, I wish to thank my
wife, Helen, who for more than thirty years has shared—
at times, endured—my *bibliomania* in addition to furnishing extremely helpful criticism and valuable aid.

EMMET FIELD HORINE, M.D.

Brooks, Kentucky
October 20, 1947, the Anniversary
of Daniel Drake's 162nd birthday.

NOTE: The reader's attention is called to Toulmin's account of
the Kentucky of 1793, published as this edition of *Pioneer Life in
Kentucky* goes to press. Without furnishing the intimate details
given by Dr. Drake in his "reminiscential letters," Toulmin's
description, written for emigrants, is remarkably corroborative.
Consult Harry Toulmin: *The Western Country in 1793...* Edited
by Marion Tinling and Godfrey Davies, [The Henry E. Hunt-
ington Library and Art Gallery] San Marino, California, 1948.

April 26, 1948   E. F. H.

BIOGRAPHICAL SKETCH

OF

DANIEL DRAKE, M. D.

(1785-1852)

O N a cold, damp and dreary day of December, 1800,
fifteen year old Daniel Drake, a timid, home-loving
country boy from Kentucky, was brought by his father
to the home of the leading physician of Cincinnati, Ohio.
Here *Dannel* was to remain four years and be "transmuted"
into a doctor. Forty-five years later, he reminiscences:
"Father remained a day, when to my dismay, he took leave
of me, and I took to **Chesselden's** Anatomy."[1]

The realization of his inadequate preparation for the
study of medicine no doubt stimulated Drake to the utmost. Puzzling technical terms derived from Greek and
Latin, of which he then knew nothing, constantly con-
fronted him. With a zeal that must have surprised and
delighted his teacher, he persevered. In Letter VII, mention
is made of his occupancy of a room with other boys in the
home of Dr. William Goforth, his preceptor. Elsewhere,
Dr. Drake intimates that, at times, he slept underneath

[1] Letter X, Note 9, page 246.

the "greasy counter" of the apothecary shop with the "olfactory nerves [regaled] in the mingled odors which, like incense to the god of Physic, rose from brown paper bundles, bottles stopped with worm-eaten corks, and open jars of ointment, not a whit behind those of the Apothecary in the days of Solomon."[2]

Daniel Drake was the first student of medicine in Cincinnati and, after his apprenticeship, was given by Dr. Goforth (August 1, 1805) a *diploma* which read: "I do certify, that Mr. Daniel Drake has pursued under my direction, for four years, the study of Physic, Surgery, and Midwifery. From his good Abilities and marked Attention to the Prosecution of his studies, I am fully convinced, that he is well qualified to practice in the above branches of his Profession." At this time, Dr. Goforth took him into partnership.

In October, 1805, Drake went on horseback, a journey of eighteen days over the mountains, to Philadelphia to take his first formal course of lectures in the Medical Department of the University of Pennsylvania. Returning in April, 1806, he practiced for a year at his Kentucky home, Mayslick. In the meantime, Dr. Goforth had decided to leave Cincinnati and, possibly at his suggestion, Dr. Drake located there.

Drake quickly acquired a large practice and entered into active participation in many civic enterprises. He was a member of the first debating society, helped establish the first dramatic group and was chairman of the first committee which proposed a circulating library in Cincinnati.

---

[2] Daniel Drake: *Discourses Delivered by Appointment before the Cincinnati Medical Library Association* . . . (Cincinnati, 1852), page 55.

He was welcomed as a member of the small, though highly intellectual social set of the then rapidly expanding village. On December 20, 1807, Dr. Drake was married to Miss Harriet Sisson, a niece of Col. Jared Mansfield, Surveyor-General of the Northwest Territory. Harriet Sisson was a beautiful, talented and resourceful young woman, a worthy companion for the highly talented and ambitious young physician.

On July 22, 1807, Drake sent a communication to *The Philadelphia Medical and Physical Journal,* which was edited by one of his former professors, Dr. Benjamin Smith Barton. This initial article, unusual in its clarity and conciseness, was entitled *Some Account of the Epidemic Diseases which prevail at Mays-Lick in Kentucky.*[3] In a brief and logical manner he described an epidemic, probably typhoid fever, which had occurred at Mayslick in the autumn of 1806.

His second publication was a pamphlet of 64 pages, *Notices concerning Cincinnati.*[4] Printed in 1810, it has a botanical section which contains the earliest listing of the indigenous plants. This booklet was so well received that Dr. Drake soon began assembling material for a much larger work to describe, not only Cincinnati, but also the whole Miami River region of Ohio in a most comprehensive manner. After considerable unavoidable delay, the result

[3] Daniel Drake: *Some Account of the Epidemic Diseases which Prevail at Mays-Lick in Kentucky,* The Philadelphia Medical and Physical Jour., Vol. III (Part I): 85-90, 1808.

[4] Daniel Drake: *Notices concerning Cincinnati,* (Cincinnati, John W. Browne & Co., 1810.)

of the failure to obtain delivery of the maps from the east, the greatly enlarged book, *Natural and Statistical View, or Picture of Cincinnati and the Miami Country* . . . was ready for sale in February 1816. It gained renown for its author throughout the United States and even abroad.

In the meantime Drake spent the winter and spring of 1815-16 in Philadelphia pursuing his second course of lectures at the University of Pennsylvania. He was graduated with the degree of M.D., at a convocation especially called for this purpose, on May 11, 1816. He resumed his practice in Cincinnati the following June 18.

It is not surprising that the Trustees of Transylvania University, Lexington, Kentucky, offered him, in 1817, the Chair of Materia Medica and Medical Botany. He accepted and thus became the first professor of these subjects as well as a member of the first active medical faculty west of the Allegheny Mountains. This was the beginning of his career as an educator, which vocation he followed, with brief interruptions, until his death.[5]

Dissension arose in the medical faculty — Dr. Benjamin W. Dudley and William H. Richardson quarreled throughout the session and Drake resigned at its close. Dudley then accused Drake of breach of faith in addition to many charges of lesser importance. Drake issued a defense in pamphlet form addressed to the *Intelligent and Respectable People of Lexington* (1818) in which, with unanswerable logic, he refuted all charges. Some biographers of

[5] Emmet Field Horine: *Daniel Drake and his Contributions to Education*, The Papers of the Bibliographical Society of America, Vol. XXXIV: 303-314, 1940.

Drake have erroneously asserted that he refused to accept a challenge to a duel. Contemporary sources disclose that Drake was not challenged but boldly announced his positive intention of accepting any challenge proffered. Probably Dudley had had enough of duelling, having shortly before Drake's retort, fought with pistols in response to the challenge of William H. Richardson.

Returning to Cincinnati and his practice in 1818, having proved beyond question his unusual teaching ability, he began a series of public lectures on botany. The editorial comment of *The Western Spy*[6] is interesting:

A course of Botanical Lectures for the coming season, was commenced on Friday evening 8th inst. [May 1818] by Dr. Drake, with an introductory Lecture of much interest. It is truly gratifying to see so numerous and respectable an audience at the first attempt of the kind in the Western Country . . .

During the fall and winter of 1818, Dr. Drake with two associates delivered a course of medical lectures which attracted more students than ever before assembled for a similar purpose in the West. The success of the undertaking prompted Drake to inaugurate plans for the incorporation of a medical college. By personal solicitation before the General Assembly he succeeded in having The Medical College of Ohio duly incorporated on January 19, 1819.[7]

[6] [Editorial] — Botanical Lectures, *The Western Spy* (Cincinnati, Ohio), Vol. IV (New Series), May 16, 1818, page (3), column (1).

[7] Ohio — *Acts of the General Assembly*, (Chillicothe: Geo. Nashee, 1819), Vol. 17, pages 37-40.

At the same session of the Ohio General Assembly, Drake was instrumental in having incorporated CincinnatiCollege to which further reference is made. This institution was empowered to "grant and confer on any candidate, in such form as they may direct, all or any of the degrees that are usually conferred in any college or university of the United States."[8] The Cincinnati College, of which Drake was a Trustee, was to manage the affairs of the Cincinnati Lancaster Seminary of which he also was a Trustee. His activities at this time for the advancement of Cincinnati made him its foremost citizen and physician. He was the founder and one of the managers of the Western Museum, a Vice-President of the Humane Society, a Director of the United States Branch Bank, President of the Cincinnati Library Society, a member of the Standing Committee of the Cincinnati Society for the Promotion of Agriculture and President of The Medical College of Ohio.[9]

For a distinguished visitor to come to Cincinnati without a letter of introduction to Dr. Drake was unusual. Even without a formal introduction visitors were welcomed by him. Space prevents the enumeration of the many persons of distinction who came to Cincinnati and who were accorded the "greatest civility" by Drake. Elsewhere (Letter III, Note 9) reference has been made to the distinguished Englishwoman, Harriet Martineau, and her tribute to him. Among the notables visiting Cincinnati, Frances Trollope is almost alone in her failure to make mention of Drake.

[8] Ohio — *Acts of the General Assembly*, (Chillicothe: Geo. Nashee, 1819), Vol. 17, pages 46-50.

[9] *The Cincinnati [Ohio] Directory*, Oliver Farnsworth, October, 1819, pages 37, 39, 40, 45, 47, 97, and 151.

Edward Thomson (1810-1870), physician, later Bishop of the Methodist Church and President of Ohio Wesleyan College states:

... [Dr. Drake's] social qualities were remarkable. His acquaintance being extensive, his threshold was often crossed by guests, whom he always treated hospitably. Indeed, his house was almost always open; and whenever a notable stranger was in the city, it was usually the scene of a party ... [10]

Dr. Drake's inability to secure a competent faculty and open his medical college in November, 1819, was a bitter disappointment. He continued his efforts and finally on August 20, 1820, was able to announce the organization of the college with a full faculty.[11] On November 11, 1820, this second school west of the Alleghenies opened with a class of 24 students. At this time, President Drake delivered *An Inaugural Discourse on Medical Education.* Among other noteworthy recommendations was an extension to five months of the course of medical study in lieu of the four months' session then the accepted plan in all existing medical schools in the United States. Broader preliminary education, bedside teaching and hospital training were advocated. I have italicized the following quotation in which he insisted that the student must *not* confine his researches to the structural changes alone but "... *must*

[10] E. Thomson: *Sketches, Biographical and Incidental,* Edited by Rev. D. W. Clark, (Cincinnati: L. Swormstedt & A. Poe, 1856), page 113.
[11] [Advertisement] — *Liberty Hall and Cincinnati Gazette,* Vol. 2 (New Series), August 23, 1820, page (3), columns (2-3).

extend them to the mind itself, and to its operations and effects."[12]

Ever active, Drake in 1821 was instrumental in having the General Assembly of Ohio charter the Commercial Hospital and Lunatic Asylum at Cincinnati. Initially the plan to found this institution met with considerable opposition. Gen. Wm. Henry Harrison, friend and patient of Dr. Drake, intervened and so influenced the Assembly that the law creating the hospital was enacted. This was the first hospital in the Mississippi Valley established for teaching purposes, staffed only by the professors of a medical school. Drake declared:

. . . The laboratory is not more necessary for the study of chemistry or a garden of plants for the study of botany, than a hospital for the study of practical medicine and surgery . . . [13]

His ability and personality were so clearly superior that jealousies were inevitable. At the close of the second session of The Medical College of Ohio, two members of the faculty resigned and Drake, the founder, was expelled! In a pamphlet issued May 1, 1822, he delineates the scene:

. . . A profound silence ensued, our dim taper shed a blue light over the lurid faces of the plotters, and every thing seemed ominous of an approaching revolution. On trying occasions, Dr. Smith is said to be subject to a disease not unlike Saint Vitus'

[12] Daniel Drake: *An Inaugural Discourse on Medical Education*. . . (Cincinnati, Ohio: Looker, Palmer and Reynolds, 1820.), page 8.

[13] Daniel Drake: *Introductory Lecture at the Opening of the Thirtieth Session of the Medical College of Ohio,* Nov. 5, 1849. (Cincinnati: Morgan and Overend, 1849), p. 15.

Dance; and on this he did not wholly escape. Wan and trembling he raised himself (with the exception of his eyes) and in lugubrious accents said, "Mr. President — In the resolution I am about to offer, I am influenced by no *private feelings,* but solely by a reference to the public good." He then read as follows: "Voted that Daniel Drake, M. D. be dismissed from the Medical College of Ohio." The portentous stillness recurred, and was not interrupted till I reminded the gentlemen of their designs. Mr. Slack, who is blessed with stronger nerves than his master, then rose, and adjusting himself to a firmer balance, put on a proper sanctimony, and bewailingly ejaculated, "I second the motion." The crisis had now manifestly come; and learning by enquiry that the gentlemen were ready to meet it, I put the question, which carried, in the classical language of Dr. Smith, *"nemo contradiscente."* I could not do more than tender them a vote of thanks, nor less than withdraw, and performing both, the Doctor politely lit me down stairs . . . [14]

As a result of indignation and the demands of leading citizens, he was reinstated the following week but immediately resigned.

Transylvania University again offered him a chair and he accepted. Here he taught four years and was elected Dean of the Faculty. During his incumbency, Transylvania enrolled the largest medical class in its history. Drake's second period (1823-1827) in Lexington resulted in the development of a lifelong friendship with Henry Clay. When, in 1825, the charge of a corrupt deal between John Quincy Adams and Clay was made by George Kremer and

[14] Daniel Drake: *A Narrative of the Rise and Fall of The Medical College of Ohio,* (Cincinnati, Ohio, 1822, Looker & Reynolds), pages 10-11.

Andrew Jackson, Drake valiantly defended Clay in letters to newspapers which received much publicity.

Resigning from his position in Lexington, he returned (1827) to Cincinnati where he founded *The Western Medical and Physical Journal, Original and Eclectic*. Edited with the ability evidenced in all his other endeavors, this periodical was continued for almost thirty years. In this *Journal* his famous essays on medical education first appeared which were republished with additions in book format.[15] At the time of their publication these remarkable essays did not attract the attention they deserved, probably because they were so many decades ahead of the time. Col. Fielding H. Garrison (1870-1935), medical historian and one-time Librarian of the U. S. Army Medical Library, believed these essays were "the most important contributions ever made on the subject in this country."[16] Otto Juettner (1865-1922), physician and medical biographer of Cincinnati, said:

They are typical of the man, earnest, animated and permeated throughout by an idealism that is inspiring. The diction is matchless.[17]

Of western physicians, Daniel Drake was the first to be called to a professorship in an eastern school. In 1830 he

[15] Daniel Drake: *Practical Essays on Medical Education and the Medical Profession* . . . (Cincinnati, Ohio: Roff & Young, 1832.)

[16] Fielding H. Garrison: *An Introduction to the History of Medicine* . . . 3rd Ed., (Philadelphia: W. B. Saunders Co., 1924), page 465.

[17] Otto Juettner: *Daniel Drake and his Followers*, (Harvey Publishing Co., Cincinnati [1909]), page 76.

was offered and accepted the Chair of the Theory and Practice of Medicine in the Jefferson Medical College at Philadelphia. Though enthusiastically received he remained only one session and then returned to his beloved Cincinnati where he still hoped to establish an outstanding medical school, Miami University, Medical Department, 1831. The Trustees of The Medical College of Ohio realizing that such competition would ruin the prospects of their institution, sought a compromise. This was finally arranged, Drake being able to secure certain concessions. No sooner had a truce been declared than internal dissensions arose resulting in his resignation. Thereupon, he devoted himself to his extensive practice, to his numerous private pupils, to his editorial duties and other literary endeavors.

Drake's interest in education continued and, in 1835, he was able to resuscitate (with medical and law departments) the Cincinnati College which he had fathered in 1819. The Medical Department, with Drake as Dean, had one of the most distinguished faculties ever assembled in the West. During the four years of its existence, more students were attracted to it than to its rival. Despite this fact, the lack of any endowment forced its closure and Drake's ceaseless efforts were thus again doomed to failure.

William J. Barbee (1816-1892), a pupil of Dr. Drake at approximately this time, has said:

As a professor, Dr. Drake, in my estimation, is not second to any man in the United States. I have always associated him with Rush . . . [Dr. Drake's] style of lecturing is easy and pleasant; and for the purpose of riveting more closely the attention of all within his hearing, he will often stop, and under pretext of ignorance, ask some one present information respecting some anatomical fact. His lectures are not unfrequently spiced with wit and humor . . . [18]

Another of his students, Dr. David W. Yandell (1826-1898), President of the American Medical Association in 1872, said:

. . . As a lecturer Dr. Drake had few equals. He was never dull. His was an alert and masculine mind. His words were full of vitality. His manner was earnest and impressive. His eloquence was fervid . . . [19]

On September 7, 1839, Drake was unanimously elected Professor of Clinical Medicine and Pathological Anatomy, a chair especially created for him, in the Louisville Medical Institute (now the School of Medicine, University of Louisville). Apparently he was happy in Louisville where he remained ten years.

Between courses of lectures he traveled extensively (covering possibly 30,000 miles) through lower Canada, the lake region, the Mississippi Valley and the southern states. While his primary purpose was to obtain first-hand information relative to the diseases of the inhabitants, he was interested in everything he saw. He observed particularly the methods of teaching in the medical colleges, mak-

[18] W. J. B[arbee]: *Letters from the West*—No. V, *The Boston Med. and Surg. Jour.*, Vol. XXI: 96-98, September 18, 1839.

[19] David W. Yandell: *The Doctorate Address Delivered at the Semi-Centennial Anniversary of the University of Louisville . . .*, (Louisville: J. P. Morton & Co., 1887.)

ing note of their libraries and other equipment. He often carried on his editorial duties during the summer months by writing letters for his journal which were labeled *Traveling Memoranda,* sometimes *Traveling Editorials.* In one of them he said:

The period of greatest usefulness, in the life of a physician, extends from 40 to 60 — he is not a man of wisdom before the former, nor of energy, after the latter term.[20]

These letters contained sprightly accounts of the many things he saw and, at times, might be considered gossipy.

By this time Drake's reputation was a national one and patients from considerable distances often consulted him. His practice became largely consultative. In 1841, Abraham Lincoln wrote to Drake describing an illness at length and asking for an opinion particularly with reference to treatment. Dr. Drake "refused to give either without personal examination."[21]

To Drake's suggestion should be credited the establishment of the Kentucky School for the Blind in Louisville on May 5, 1842. During the winter of 1841-42, he delivered a series of popular lectures on physiology in which he discussed the different methods of teaching the blind, and urged that a school be opened for them in Kentucky. One of his hearers soon after introduced in the Legislature a

[20] Daniel Drake: [Editorial] — *Traveling Memoranda, Western Journal of the Medical and Physical Sciences,* (Cincinnati) Second Hexade, Vol. IV:311-319, July, August and September 1836.

[21] Albert J. Beveridge: *Abraham Lincoln, 1809-1858,* 2 Vols. (Boston: Houghton Mifflin Co., 1928), Vol. I: 312-313.

bill for this purpose, which was passed.[22] The school thus created has continued in successful operation up to the present time.

During Dr. Drake's years in Louisville, there was completed the whole of the first volume of his masterpiece: *A Systematic Treatise, Historical, Etiological, and Practical on the Principal Diseases of the Interior Valley of North America, as they appear in the Caucasian, African, Indian and Esquimaux Varieties of its Population.* This was published in 1850 and a second volume in 1854. At the Cincinnati meeting of the American Medical Association in 1850, Dr. Alfred Stillé in his report on recent medical literature stated:

... It belongs to the very highest rank of our medical literature, and may very probably come to be regarded as the most valuable original work yet published in America ... Its distinguished author has raised a durable monument to his own name, and to the medical reputation, not only of the Great Valley, but to the greater Union ... [23]

Garrison said of Drake's *Treatise*:

... There was nothing like this book in literature, unless it might be Hippocrates on Airs, Waters, and Places, and even Hippocrates made no attempt to map out or triangulate the geographic locale of disease ... [24]

[22] Daniel Drake: [Editorial] — *Kentucky School for the Instruction of the Blind, Western Journal of Med. and Surg.,* (Louisville), Vol. V:237, March 1842.

[23] Alfred Stillé: [Chairman] — Committee on Medical Literature [for 1849-50], *Transactions of the American Medical Assn.,* (Philadelphia, 1850), Vol. III:166.

[24] Garrison, op. cit., page 465.

Because of the critical state of The Medical College of Ohio, Drake was recalled in 1849 and triumphantly received by the institution he had founded. Dissension arose during the session. At its close, he resigned and returned to Louisville. In 1852 he was again urged to come to the rescue in Cincinnati, and with that unexplainable filial love for a most unappreciative and erring child, Drake acquiesced. Reaching Cincinnati in October, 1852, he became ill but, despite his indisposition, began lectures preliminary to his regular course.

He accepted an invitation to attend a meeting of the Kentucky State Medical Society at Louisville on October 20, 1852, where he was elected an honorary member.[25] Returning to Cincinnati on October 25th he continued, for the next three days, his usual routine of prescribing for patients at the hospital, lecturing and writing. After this he became too ill to leave his residence, and growing steadily weaker, died at 6:00 P.M. on November 5, 1852. He was buried in Spring Grove Cemetery, Cincinnati, beside his beloved Harriet who had died September 30, 1825.

Dr. Samuel D. Gross, in whose parlor Dr. Drake paraded (Letter VIII), was associated with him in teaching for fifteen years. He said of him:

. . . As a colleague or companion no man could have been more agreeable, more considerate, or more honorable. Most of the difficulties and annoyances which beset him in his younger days are attributable to his connection with the Medical Col-

---

[25] *Transactions of the Kentucky State Medical Society*, October 1852, (Louisville, Ky., Webb & Levering, 1853), page 16.

lege of Ohio, and to the fact, everywhere patent, that he generally was greatly in advance of his collaborators in his attempts to improve medical education and to build up a successful school, the idol for many years of his professional life. Drake had nothing bad in him; his faults were errors of judgment, not errors of the heart, which was always in the right place . . . [26]

In this necessarily brief summary of the life of Drake, I have alluded to only a few of his numerous contributions to medical literature. His style was clear, concise, vigorous and even, at times, poetic. One of his most beautifully descriptive essays is *The Northern Lakes, a Summer Resort for Invalids of the South*.[27] With a moving and artistic touch he pictures the lake region, methods and routes of travel, principal cities and scenic grandeur.

Not only was he a leader in all medical affairs but also in civic enterprises, both numerous and diverse. We must enthusiastically concur with William H. Venable (1836-1920), Ohio teacher, author, editor and historian when he says of Drake:

So many good works did he undertake, so much did he accomplish, so effectually did he stimulate exertion in others, both friends and enemies, that I think he may be called with propriety the *Franklin of Cincinnati* . . . [28]

[26] Samuel D. Gross: *Autobiography,* 2 Vols. (Philadelphia: George Barrie, 1887), Vol. II, page 272.

[27] Daniel Drake: *The Northern Lakes, a Summer Resort for Invalids of the South, The Western Jour. of Med. and Surg.,* (Louisville, Ky.), Vol. VI:401-426, December 1842.

[28] W. H. Venable: *Beginnings of Literary Culture in the Ohio Valley* . . . , (Cincinnati: Robert Clarke & Co., 1891), page 304.

Doctor Drake has been accused of being quarrelsome but I have yet to find a single instance, in any dispute, in which he was the aggressor. In controversies, his keen sense of humor combined with a remarkable proficiency in the use of invective proved devastating to those who dared attack him or the causes he held dear. Further, once attacked, he showed no quarter but argued so logically, so convincingly, and, indeed at times, with such persistence that he was almost invariably victorious.

As the years pass and as a truer perspective of the first half of the nineteenth century in American Medicine becomes possible, the fame of Daniel Drake will increase. An intensely patriotic citizen, a philanthropist, a philosopher and teacher as well as author and editor, a zealous and assiduous worker, a modest and unassuming genius with lofty ideals and laudable ambition, A TRUE PHYSICIAN was the immortal Daniel Drake.

CONTENTS

ILLUSTRATIONS

TREK FROM NEW JERSEY
TO MAYSLICK

THE SETTING

Dr. Drake's conclusion in Letter I that the tide of immigration to Kentucky was remarkable is correct. The first cabin in what is now Kentucky was erected by the surveyor and physician, Dr. Thomas Walker, in 1750. In 1774 several cabins were built at Harrodsburg and in various other sections of the county. By 1775 the population did not exceed a few hundred. In 1784 Filson (*The Discovery, Settlement and Present State of Kentacke...* Wilmington, 1784, page 28) estimated that there were 30,000 inhabitants. The first U.S. census in 1790 gave Kentucky a population of 73,577 and the second (1800), 220,955!

There were a number of motives which accounted for this spectacular migration to the West. Land was relatively cheap and an inhabitant of one of the Atlantic states could sell his hundred acres there and acquire, in Kentucky, over a thousand far more fertile ones and have a substantial sum remaining. The desire for adventure or for acquisition of riches in a newly developing territory doubtless played a part. Some there were, probably, who wished to escape prosecution either for debt or crime. Taxes were high in the Seaboard states after the Revolution, and they could be avoided by emigration. The climate was milder than in the more northerly Atlantic states though this deterred at least one Pennsylvania German as reported by Schoepf (Travels in the Confederation, 1783-1784, A. J. Morrison translation, Philadelphia, 1911, Vol. II, p. 5): "He had heard that in Kentucky there is no real winter; and where there is no winter, he argued, people must work year in, year out, and that was not his fancy; winter, with a warm stove and sluggish days, being indispensable to his happiness."

Letter One

TREK FROM NEW JERSEY TO MAYSLICK

To Harriet Echo[1]

Louisville, [Kentucky]
Dec[r] 15, 1847 — 10 P.M.

Two hours more, my dear Harriet, will complete 47 years since I left the log cabin of my father and the arms of my mother, to engage in the study of medicine in the Village of Cincinnati, often, at that time called Fort Washington. [Two years ago], on the anniversary of my departure, I took it into my head to give your sister an off hand sketch of that (to the family and myself) memorable event, and of my journey, and introduction into the family of D[r] Goforth.[2] Such, at least, is my recollection of the scope of my letter[3] which I suppose you saw, for I intended it, as I do the one which I have now begun, to be a sort of family record...

[1] Harriet Echo, youngest of five children of Daniel and Harriet (Sisson) Drake. Their first child, a girl christened Harriet, died in infancy hence the name Harriet *Echo*. At the time this letter was written, she was Mrs. James Parker Campbell.

[2] Dr. William Goforth (1766-1817), a native of New York, practiced his profession at Washington, Ky., from 1788 to 1799. He was the physician, adviser and friend to the families comprising the Mayslick settlement. In 1799, he removed to Cincinnati where he remained until 1807, when he went to Louisiana. Returning to Cincinnati in 1816, he died the following year.

[3] Letter X, page 235.

I was prompted to write that letter, and am incited to undertake this, by the feeling that if I had (now that my honored parents are gone, as I hope and trust, to the abode of the redeemed) a written record of their early lives, it would be to me a most precious document. I may anticipate, then, that when you and the rest of my dear and devoted children have reached my age and I have been long gone to join my parents, as I humbly hope to do, you will feel the kind of interest concerning me, in every stage of my life, that I feel in reference to them. . . I fear however, [that these reminiscences] will, through the period to which this letter relates, be found both meagre and imperfect, for which, of course, there is no remedy for nearly every person who might aid me has been gathered to our fathers.

Before speaking of myself I must say something of my *ancestry*. Now one of Noah Webster's definitions of that word is, honorable descent, or the line of high birth. Were my progenitors, then, persons of fortune, learning or fame? They were not — so far from it, they were in very moderate circumstances, illiterate,[4] and unknown to fame. Still I stick to the word, for as far as I have been able to learn, they were industrious, temperate, honest, and pious, and to have sprung from *such* ancestors is *high* descent, in the sight of Heaven, if not in the estimate of men. To sustain *such* a family character is no easy task. However I may fail, I have a well founded expectation that my children will not; and

---

[4] In describing his parents as illiterate, Dr. Drake has scarcely done them justice. The ability to read and write which they admittedly possessed was exceptional in the eighteenth and early nineteenth centuries. Therefore, although their schooling was limited, they could not be called illiterate.

Harriet Echo Drake Campbell

that the line of honorable descent will be raised by them, if I should permit it to slacken.

My father, Isaac, was the youngest son of Nathaniel Drake & Dorothy Retan [Rattan]. My mother, Elizabeth, always called Betsey, was the daughter of [Benjamin] Shotwell and [Elizabeth] Bonney. They were born within three or four miles of each other, and both belonged, as [had] their ancestors . . . to the country, and were labourers on the farm. The mothers of both my parents died, and both my grand fathers were married again before my father and mother married. In reference to the children, both marriages were unhappy; and the narratives which, in childhood, I used to hear from father and mother concerning the conduct of their stepmothers, made an indelible impression upon my mind. My father had two brothers, Abraham & Cornelius, both older than himself, who married before him, while their mother was still alive, and received from their father their portion of his estate. My father never received any, which he always ascribed to the influence of his step mother.

My maternal grand father lost nearly every thing he had by purchasing and supplying the Army of the revolution with cattle for which he was paid in "Continental money," which depreciated until its value altogether vanished. Both my grandfathers lived in the very midst of the battle scenes of that revolution, and after a battle fought in the orchard of grandfather Shotwell, during which the family (and himself in bad health) retreated to the cellar, the **Brittish** entered the house, and destroyed nearly all the furniture. He himself, being of the society of *Friends,* was, of course, a noncombatant. Grandfather Drake was not; and two of his sons, including my father, if not all three, were frequently engaged in the partisan warfare of that region.

After the marriage of my parents, about the year 1783, they went to housekeeping near my grandfather Drake's, on his land where the town of Plainfield, [New Jersey], now is. He owned a small gristmill on a branch of the Raritan River called Bound-brook, and my father's occupation was "to tend" it. The first born of the family was a daughter, who was named Phebe, and died in infancy. The next in order was myself, which in some countries would have made me a miller.

My birthday, as you know, was the 20th of October, 1785. I was named for one of my mother's brothers, and at the place of my birth spent the first two and a half years of my life. Of my character and conduct during that period, tradition hath spoken rather sparingly... but three things have been handed down (with undeniable verity). They, however, were so original as to show that, sooner or later, I should be a man of some distinction... 1st I was *precocious,* and that too, in the feet, rather than the head, for when I was in my 8th month I could waddle across the cabin floor, when held up and led on by one hand. 2^{d} When older & locomotive enough to totter over the doorsill and get out on the grass, as I was sitting there one day, a mad dog came along; and what do you think I did? Strangle him, as Hercules did the two big snakes which crawled so rashly into his cradle? No; more than that! I looked at the mad animal, and he thought it prudent to pass me by, and attack a small herd of cattle, several of which died from his bite! 3^{d} As soon as I could run about I made for the mill but whether from the instinct of the anserine tribe or a leaning towards the trade of a miller, doth not appear. Whatever impulse prompted my visits, they were not without danger, and gave my mother, who had no servant, a great deal of trouble. I find it 5' after 12 o'c'k—so I must bid you *Adieu*.

Decr 16th [?] *o'c'k P.M.* I resume my narrative, hoping that a night's sleep hath prepared you for a return to it. How precious is sleep under the pressure of a long story, of which the teller is the hero!

My father and his brothers were not contented with their position, and thought of emigrating. At that time, *your* native state was the habitation of Indians only,[5] and Kentucky was but 9 years older than myself . . . [6] The brothers at first thought of moving [to Virginia]; but when two of them, including my father, made a visit there, they hesitated... The Rev. William Wood, [a Baptist minister] who a few years before had emigrated...to Kentucky, came back...and gave such glowing accounts of K^y that old Virginia was soon forgotten. The Rev. Mr Gano, of New York, another Baptist minister, or some of his sons, had

[5] Drake, in stating that Kentucky was the "habitation of Indians" is not strictly correct. With the exception of a few Shawnees dwelling along the Ohio, and a smaller number of Chickasaws in the southwestern end of the state, the region was uninhabited. However, Kentucky was a rich and prized hunting ground for the numerous tribes living to the north, west and south. Especially the Iroquois and the Cherokees laid such claim to *Kentacke* (meadow land). For its possession, they fought ferociously both among themselves and, collectively, against the settlers.

[6] The reference here is to the division of Fincastle County, Virginia, into Kentucky, Washington and Montgomery counties. It was not until 1792 that Kentucky was admitted into the Union.

visited K^y and his breath of praise still further fanned the flames — till at length the iron ties of affection for home and friends were melted, and a departure was determined upon. The decision extended to five families: - the three brothers, Mr David Morris [at times spelled by him, *Morriss*], older than either of them, who was married to my mother's cousin, and Mr John Shotwell, rather younger, who was the brother of Mrs Morris. Of the whole, my father was the youngest, the poorest, and the most limited in learning. Both he and my mother, however, could read & write, though neither of them knew any thing of grammar, geography, or arithmetic. Their reading could not have been extensive, for when I could first remember, the Bible, Rippon's Collection of hymns, the almanac, Dilworth's Spelling book, and a romance of the ages of Chivalry, entitled the "Famous history of Montellion," made up their whole library. The [last] I should greatly like to see again.

The time fixed on for their departure was the latter part of the spring of 1788. Their first point [was] Red stone Old Fort where Brownsville, [Pennsylvania], now stands. Their mode of travelling was in two horse wagons. The family of my father consisted, after himself and my mother, of myself, about 2 years & 7 months old, my sister Elizabeth, afterwards Mrs Glenn, an infant at the breast, and my mother's unmarried sister, Lydia, who chose to accompany her into the wilderness, rather than submit to the caprices of a step mother for a longer time.

Behold, then, the departure! These five persons, three of whom were adults, with all their earthly goods crowded into one "Jersey Wagon," to be hauled over the yet steep &

rugged Allegheny mountains, and throughout an overland journey of nearly 400 miles by two horses. Their travel was by Corryell's Ferry, on the Delaware, and Harris' Ferry, now Harrisburg, [Pa.], which you have visited, on the Susquehanna.

There were but few taverns on the way, and if there had been many, we should not have been much the better for them, as father's means were too limited to admit of a participation in their comforts.[7] He could only purchase necessary food, which was cooked when we stopped at night and before we started in the morning. As the weather was mild, our lodgings were often in the wagon.

In this important and difficult enterprise I no doubt played (to others) a troublesome part; but I can say nothing from memory. The only incident to which tradition testifies is, that while on the Alleghenies, when descending the steep & rocky side of a mountain, I clambered over the front board of the wagon, and hung on the outside by my hands, when I was discovered & taken in, before I had fallen, to be crushed, perhaps, by the wheels...

I know not the length of time we were in reaching Red stone Old Fort, nor how long a preparation for the voyage to the "Point" or "Limestone" now Maysville, [Ky.], detained us. When I was at (or just leaving) Mayslick nearly 3 years

[7] Aside from affording shelter from the elements, the taverns of this period offered little in the way of comfort. Many of them consisted of a single room which served for all purposes (consult Letter X, page 244). The few beds available in even the more pretentious ones usually had corn-shuck mattresses. It was customary for men, women and children to sleep, rolled in their blankets, on the floor of the public room which was heated only by a fireplace.

since, Mr Jasper Morris told me that his father had kept a diary of the journey, which was in his possession, and which I long very much to see. How many families were crowded into one boat, I do not know. The first and last landing [before reaching Limestone] was at Fort-pitt, now Pittsburg. The danger of being attacked by the Indians was too great to justify a landing [between that point and Limestone].

The flotilla, I presume, consisted of several boats, for the Rev. Mr Gano, with a numerous family, including the present Mrs Gen. Gano and her brother, Dr Wm Goforth, afterwards my preceptor, belonged to the river community. One of Mr Gano's boats got stoved, but no lives were lost. That which my parents were in met with no accident; and on the 10th of June, 1788, just 64 days after the first settlement of Ohio at Marietta, we landed at Limestone, [Ky.], which then consisted of a few [log] cabins only, though Washington, 4 miles off, was something of a Village...

Before landing, father got his ankle sprained and was unable to walk. He had to be carried out of the boat, and then could put but *one* foot on the land of promise. Who carried him I know not, but he was not very heavy; for he had in his pockets but *one* dollar, and that was asked for a bushel of corn![8] The gloom of this destitution was not as

8 Edward D. Mansfield (1801-1880), a cousin to Daniel Drake by marriage, had access to these letters prior to their first publication in 1870. In his *Memoirs of the Life and Services of Daniel Drake* ... (Cincinnati, 1855), he mentions (page 15) the arrival at Maysville of Isaac Drake with "one dollar left — which was then the price of a bushel of corn." It is amusing to observe how this statement has fired the imagination of almost every subsequent biographer of Drake. In this, as in many other respects, they have leaned heavily on Mansfield, who is frequently an untrustworthy prop.

deep to my vision, I presume, as to that of my parents and aunt; but I have no remembrance of their trials. They did not remain long at the "Point," for there were no accommodations, and the danger of Indians from the opposite side of the river was great. Washington was their first resting place.

Old Mr Gano & most of his family proceeded to Georgetown, [Ky.]. His son, John S. and Dr Goforth,... remained in Washington; the former till the 16th of November [1788], when he departed for Columbia, [Ohio], of which he was one of the first settlers..., the latter till the year 1799.

The first residence of our family was in a covered pen or shed, built for sheep adjoining the cabin of its owner. How long we continued in it I am unable to say. While occupying it, my mother one day made a call at a neighbouring cabin, where a woman was churning. Tired out with a diet of bread & meat, mother fixed her heart on a drink of buttermilk, but said nothing. When the butter was ladled out and the churn set aside, with the delicious beverage, for which she was too proud to ask (and which the other perhaps did not *think* of giving), she hastily left the house, and took a good crying spell. Thus you see whence came my propensity & Dove's & Charlie's for crying. We all in fact, resemble my mother in temperament of which this is one of the proofs while another is our hereditary propensity to go to sleep in Church!...

As father's ankle got better, he began to think of doing something; for provision had to be made for a whole year, as it was now too late to plant anything, even had there been cleared land to be planted. At that time there was a great immigration into the interior counties of Kentucky, chiefly from the state of Virginia. Lexington, settled about the year 1776[9] had in fact become already a considerable town—a kind of mart and emporium for all the infant settlements of the State, except those of the Falls [of the Ohio], where I am now writing. Consequently a considerable amount of merchandise had to be hauled to [Lexington] from Limestone, the great landing place of the state. This state of things offered employment for father, and he and Richard Ayres, the worthy father of a very unworthy son, the late Judge Ayres, of Cincinnati, determined to go to Lexington with wagon loads of goods. The enterprise was perilous, for the Indians from the north side of the river were in the habit of attacking travellers and wagoners on the road, especially north of Paris. The first night they lodged on a high hill beyond Johnson's Fork of Licking, about 14 miles from Washington; and soon after dark were alarmed by the yells of Indians! Unable or unprepared for any effective resistance, they escaped with their blankets into the bushes and crouched on the ground, leaving their wagons to be pillaged and their horses to be stolen. While lying in this unenviable condition, with no better prospect than the possible preservation of their lives, the yellers came so near as to convince them that the sounds were not human. Although neither had ever seen or heard a wolf, they decided (no doubt correctly) that a pack was near them, and returned to their fire as the safest place. When they reached Bryant's station, 5 m. from Lexington, they greatly needed bread, as their diet was almost entirely game, eaten

---

[9] The exact date of the founding of Lexington was April 17, 1779.

sometimes without salt. They applied to old M[r] Rogers, the father of my *quondam* friend, the Doctor[10] now living 3 squares from where I sit, and father purchased a piece of "**Jonny** cake" as large as his two hands, for which he paid "one & six pence," or twenty five cents.[11]

Delivering their goods, and receiving pay, a new era commenced. They had means, and were where they could purchase. And, returning they brought back, to the great joy of their families, meal, butter, cheese, tea, sugar, and other articles of sustenance—regarded as luxuries of the most delicate kind. Thus father, who began his career as a farmer, was afterwards a miller, and now a wagoner, or common carrier on the highway. It does not appear, however, that he repeated the trip; for as the fall came on, the crops around Washington ripened, and he was called, moreover, to another occupation.

From the day of the landing of the little colony (composed of the three Drakes & Shotwell & Morris) the older and more intelligent men had been casting about for a tract of land, which they might purchase, and divide among themselves. At length they fixed upon a *"settlement & preemption"* . . . 8 miles from Washington on the Lexington road. Hard by the latter, there was a salt spring, and the deer and buffalo were in the habit, as at other salt springs,

---

[10] Doctor Coleman Rogers (1781-1855) was associated with Dr. Drake for a short time at Cincinnati in 1818-19.

[11] Kentucky hospitality was such that strangers were entertained in private homes without charge. In fact, any offer of payment for food would have given offence (consult Humphrey Marshall: *The History of Kentucky*, Frankfort, 1812, page 150.) Hence this payment for the johnny-cake (journey-cake) would seem to indicate that Mr. Rogers kept a tavern.

of "licking" the surrounding earth. This tract, of 1400 acres, they purchased from a man by the name of May,[12] and decided on calling their "new home" Mayslick—a decision sufficiently indicative of uncultivated taste.

(I must stop and mend my pen during which you will have time to breathe, or wake up, as when an orator stops.)

The purchase being made, the next thing was to divide the tract, and give to each of the five a portion equal to his means of payment. That of my father was 38 acres![13] which I believe he afterwards contrived to augment to 50. How he paid even for this small participation, I am unable to state; most likely by selling his wagon and one of his horses. Desiring to live so near each other that no house, in the event of being attacked by Indians, would be unsupported by some other, they decided that every subdivision should have an angle or corner in the salt lick. A brook crossed the road near to it, running from west to east, and the three brothers built on the north side of the little stream. This building now gave occupation to all who could wield an axe; for the colony was to winter here, and autumn was upon them. As the distance was too great from Washington to permit their returning there in the evening to lodge,

[12] William May had first staked out the tract which later came into the possession of Judge Harry Innes (1752-1816) from whom the purchase was made "on or about" July 15, 1788. The details are amplified in the editor's biography of Dr. Daniel Drake now in preparation.

[13] It was not until August 24, 1790, that Isaac Drake was able to make a final payment and obtain a deed to the tract of 38¼ acres which he had bargained for in 1788.

their practice was, after supping, to retire into the woods, and lodge separately among the cane, which flourished in great luxuriance beneath the parti-colored canopy of autumnal leaves. In this way, they expected to elude the Indians. No attack was made upon them either by night or day.

Before winter set in, their rude cabins, each with its port holes and a strong bar across the door, were completed. The roofs were of clap-boards, and the floors of puncheons, for sawing was out of the question. Another and, to nearly the whole colony, the last removal took place. Kentucky was no longer a promise, but a possession — not an imagination, but a reality. They had ceased to be Jerseymen, and become Virginians; for at that time the daughter was still a member of her mother's house.

Now fancy to yourself a log cabin of the size and form of Dove's [his daughter's] dining room — one story high — without a window — with a door opening to the south — with a half finished wooden chimney — with a roof on one side only — without any upper or lower floor — and fancy, still further, a man and two women stepping from sleeper to sleeper (poles laid down to support the floor, when [my father] should find time to split the puncheons), with two children — a brother & sister — sitting on the ground between them, as joyous as you ever saw... and you will have the picture which constitutes *my first memory*. The mordant which gave permanence to the tints of this domestic scene was a sharp rebuke from my father, for making a sort of whooping, guttural noise (which is still ringing in my ears), for the amusement of my sister Lizy, then I believe about a year old, while I was a little rising three. Thus, my first memory includes an act of discipline by my father; and well would it have been for many who have grown up unimpelled and uncontrolled by parental admonition, if they had been subjected in due time to a parental sway as firm and gentle as that which presided over my childhood.

My Dear Echo, when I began this letter, I supposed that before I reached its 15th page, I should reach the events of my 15th year, when I left the roof of my devoted parents to begin the study of medicine but, behold, I have only gotten through a fifth part of that period. I have merely finished my *traditional* narrative; have but reached the era of **reminescence** — a good evidence, I think, that in mental feelings and tastes, I am a little way in the epoch of garrulous old age. At the rate I have advanced, the recollections of the next 12 years would make a little volume notwithstanding I am far from having a tenacious historical memory. To write them down would be to me a pleasure *per se;* and the thought that they might afford any gratification to you, to [my other children] and the dear grandchildren would give the undertaking much additional interest. At some future time I may, perhaps, address such a narrative to some one of you...

We had no mail boat today up to 1 o'c'k. I have not visited the P.O. since. At 10 this morning, the river was only 4½ feet below its height in 1832. The front of the city exhibits an aspect of great desolation. Shippingport & most of Portland are under water. The Snow is one of the deepest I have ever seen in Kentucky...

Cabin similar to the one erected by Isaac Drake

My introductory lecture is out today.[14] I will bring up some copies, when I visit you — starting (D.V.) on thursday next...

My love and kisses to all the dear stereotypes, retaining for yourself a full proportion.

Should I not read and correct my running, rapidly running epistle, you will not, I hope, think it strange. It would be no enviable task, to travel a second time, over 16 dull & inaccurately written pages.

Your loving Pa.

[14] In this lecture entitled, *Strictures on some of the Defects and Infirmities of Intellectual and Moral Character in Students of Medicine,* Dr. Drake, in closing, begs the students to strive to enlarge the boundaries of science and discontinue their dependence upon European thought.

THE FIRST SIX YEARS

The danger from Indian raids, stressed in the following letter, was a very real one. There were many Indian villages across the river in the region to the north which is now part of the State of Ohio. Under cover of darkness, it was easy for a band of these savages to paddle across the Ohio River in canoes which were hidden at the water's edge. Ordinarily a scout, who had preceded, was waiting to guide them to some unprotected cabin or barnyard. Scalps were prized possessions and rarely was any mercy shown. Horses were particularly desirable booty as they could be ridden to the river and then forced to swim across. It is surprising that Drake, in writing of this period, makes no mention here of the noted Indian fighter and self-appointed protector of the settlers, Simon Kenton, especially in view of the fact that he lived within a few miles of Mayslick. Kenton was ever on the alert to organize volunteer forces for retaliatory measures against the Indians.

In 1793 the situation had become so critical that an army of about 4000, under General Anthony Wayne, was sent to subdue the savages. On August 20, 1794, at the battle of Fallen Timbers, the Indians were badly defeated. Later a peace treaty was signed and a vast territory was ceded to the United States. The Indians gave to Wayne the name of *Wind* because he "was exactly like a hurricane that drives, and tears and prostrates everything before it."

Letter Two

THE FIRST SIX YEARS

To Charles Daniel Drake[1]

Louisville, [Kentucky]
Dec[r] 17th, 1847 — P.M. 3 o'c'k.

My dear Son:

There are events in our lives of such moment, that when the anniversary of their occurrence returns, the memory of them seems to bring with it the memory of many others, no way connected with them but in the continued consciousness of the individual. The same is true of nations, or the national mind. When the anniversary of the battle of Saratoga or Trenton comes round, if we notice it at all, our range of thought on the war of the Revolution is quite limited; but on the 4th of July, we are incited to a review of the causes, events and consequences of that war.

---

[1] Charles Daniel (1811-1892), the second child of Dr. Drake, who wrote a biographical sketch of his father which served as an introduction to the first publication (1870) of *Pioneer Life in Kentucky*. Impetuous and self-willed as a child and during his brief career as a midshipman, he later, in St. Louis, became a successful lawyer and author. He interested himself in Missouri state politics and, in 1867, was elected to the Senate of the United States. He resigned this office to accept, from President Grant, the Chief Justiceship of the United States Court of Claims. In accepting, he retired from politics and served as Chief Justice with distinction until his retirement in 1885.

The lives of different persons, however, are very unlike each other as to the range of comparative importance in what they do, or what happens to them. Thus, some die at three score years & ten, on the spots where they were born having, throughout the whole period, been subjected to nearly the same influences and engaged in the same pursuits. This is the case with the apprentice who becomes a mechanic, and succeeds his master, conducting the business in the place and mode of his predecessor, till he himself is superseded... [So it is] with the son of a farmer, who inherits the homestead, and cultivates it as his father before him had done. There are others, however, whose paths are eccentric, and they pass out of the orbits of their ancestors, are subjected to new influences, both attractive & repulsive. [They may] finally lose all visible connection with the states of society in which they were respectively born & reared. In the lives of such, there must of necessity be decisions, actions and events of great *relative* importance.

In my own life, my departure from the home of my father for the study of medicine was the governing event. When the anniversary of that act comes round, it calls up a multitude of reminiscences, by no means limited to the act itself, but ranging far up and down the chronometer of my life. It was the 16 th day of December when I started; this day, the 17 th I entered the State of Ohio and tomorrow will be the anniversary of my arrival in Cincinnati... The 20 th [was] the day on which I began my medical studies 47 years ago, and also the day of my marriage, seven years afterwards. Thus, you see I am in the midst of my greatest

Charles Daniel Drake

feeling into which it precipitates me deeper and deeper I find with each rolling year.

Under this influence I was prompted in 1845 or 6, to give your sister Dove an off hand sketch of some of the circumstances connected with my departure from home. When the annual exacerbation returned, two days ago, I was prompted to address to your sister Echo, a letter... containing a traditional narrative of the events in father's family through the first three years of my life. At the close of that letter, I declared that I should and would dismiss from my mind the matters, a part of which were embodied in its 15 pages but when I ordered them out, they "wouldn't go." Even while before my class, engaged in delivering an *extempore* lecture on pleurisy, they still hovered round; and as soon as I left the university,[2] began to gambol before me as friskily as a troop of **faries** in the nectary of a blue violet. I saw then that I had no resource but to drown them in ink, and lay them out to dry on paper, like butterflies in the cabinet of the entomologist. This I have now undertaken to do; but as drowned **faries** are not so fair as the living, nor dead butterflies so beautiful as those which are swarming in the beams of the summer sun, so, I am quite sure, you will find my delineations very far inferior to the images which memory has called into existence. And, still there are relations in life—those of parents & children, of husband & wife, of brother & sister, of friend & friend—which give impor-

---

[2] When this letter was written, Dr. Drake was Professor of Pathology and the Practice of Medicine in the Medical Department of the University of Louisville.

tance, and even sanctity to the smallest events and humblest actions...

The first event I can remember I have described in my letter to Harriet Echo. It occurred in the autumn or beginning of the winter of 1788 when I had entered my 4th year. For the next 6 years my father continued to reside at the same place, in the same original log cabin, which in due course of time acquired a roof, a puncheon floor below and a clap board floor above, a small square window without glass, and a chimney, carried up with *cats & clay* to the height of the ridge pole. These *cats & clay* were pieces of small poles, well imbedded in mortar. The rifle, **indespensable** both for hunting & defense, lay on two pegs driven into one of the logs. The axe and a scythe (no Jerseyman emigrated without that implement) were kept at night under the bed as weapons of defense, in case the Indians should make an attack. On the morning the first duty was to ascend a ladder which always stood, leaning behind the door, to the loft and look through the cracks for Indians lest they might have planted themselves near the door, to rush in when the strong crossbar should be removed, and the heavy latch raised from its resting place. But no attack was ever made on his or any other of the five cabins which composed the station.

The first and greatest labour after father had thus domiciliated his little family, was to clear sufficient land for a crop the following year, which was, of course, to consist of corn and a few garden vegetables. In this labour I was too young to participate, and he was too poor to hire; consequently his own hands had to perform the whole. At that time, and afterwards for more than 20 years, he was dyspeptic and by no means well fitted for the heavy task which lay before him. It was two or three years before his fields grew to any great extent. The soil, however, was highly productive and the autumn of 1789 would have brought forth a sufficient abundance but that on the night of the last day of August there came so severe a frost as to kill the unripe corn, and almost break the hearts of those who had watched its growth from day to day in joyous anticipation.

From the time of their arrival in K^y 14 months before, they had suffered from want of bread, and now found themselves doomed to the same deficiency for another year. There was no fear of famine, but they cloyed on animal food, and sometimes almost loathed it, though of excellent quality. Deer were numerous and wild **turkies** numberless. The latter were often so fat that in falling from the tree when shot their skins would burst. There was no longing for the "*flesh* pots" of native land, but their hearts yearned for its neat and abounding *wheat-bread* trays. In this craving it seems I played no unimportant part (though I do not remember it) for my parents often told me afterwards that I would cry & beg for bread when we were seated round the table till they would have to leave it & cry themselves.

During the first 3 or 4 years of our residence at Mayslick, when I was from 3 to 6 or 7 years of age, a few incidents occurred, the memory of which has not like most which transpired, vanished from my mind. But I can not arrange them chronologically, nor are they worth relating, except to children.

I well recollect that in the spring of 1790 when I was 4½

years old mother was sick and that, on a certain day, I wandered with my little sister Lizey, to whom I was always
tenderly attached, across "The Road" into the woods. We
found a tuft of yellow flowers which made so strong an impression on me that, nearly 30 years afterwards, while
studying our native botany, I recognized the same flower
and it brought up a throng of early reminiscences...

About the same period the Indians one night attacked a
body of travelers, encamped a mile from our village on the
road to Washington. They were sitting quietly around their
camp fire, when the Indians shot among them, and killed a
man whose remains I remember to have seen brought, the
next day, into the village on a rude litter. The heroic presence of mind of a woman saved the party. She broke open a
chest in one of the wagons with an axe, got at the ammunition, gave it to the men and called upon them to fight. This,
with the extinction of their Camp fires, led the Indians to
retreat.

That night made an unfading impression on my mind.
We went, with Uncle Abraham Drake's family, I think, to
Uncle Cornelius' for concentration and greater safety.
Several of the men of the village went to the relief of the
travelers and one of them, a young married man, ran into
the village and left his wife behind him! The alarm of my
mother and aunts communicated, of course, to all the
children, was deep and the remembrance of the scene was
long kept alive by talking it over & over.

Up to the victory of Wayne, in 1794, the danger from
Indians still continued; that is, through a period of six years
from the time of our arrival. I well remember that Indian

wars, midnight butcheries, captivities and horse stealings, were the daily topics of conversation. Volunteering to pursue marauding parties occasionally took place and sometimes men were drafted. This happened once to father... He hired an unmarried man as a substitute and did not go. At that time as at present, there were many young men who delighted in war much more than work and, therefore, preferred the tomahawk to the axe. I remember that when the substitute returned he had many wonderful tales to tell, but am unable to rehearse a single one...

In or near the year 1791, my aunt Lydia Shotwell was married. A number of Father's acquaintances in and around Washington were invited. They came armed, and while assembled in the house, report was brought that the Indians, about 5 miles up the Road toward Lexington, had attacked a wagon. All the armed men mounted their horses & galloped off in a style so picturesque that I shall never forget it. The alarm proved to be false.[3]

At that period, the Shawnees residing on the Scioto, & the Wyandots on the Sandusky, were our great enemies. The children were told at night, "lie still and go to sleep, or the Shawnees will catch you." When I was at the mouth of

---

[3] Dr. Drake apparently errs in stating that the alarm was false. In *Simon Kenton, His Life and Period, 1755-1836,* (Garden City, 1930), Miss Edna Kenton states (page 198) that an Indian raid interrupted the first wedding ever celebrated at Mayslick (i.e., of Dr. Drake's aunt). Miss Kenton's statement is based on careful research among the Kenton Papers in the Draper Manuscripts of the State Historical Society, Madison, Wis. According to Miss Kenton (personal communication) the correct date of the wedding was September 4, 1790.

the Kansas river in 1844 among the same tribes,[4] removed to that region and considerably civilized, the mothers, I was told, threatened their children at night with the wild Indians who lived beyond them.

Thro' the period of which I have been speaking & for several years afterwards, as I well recollect, nearly all my troubled or vivid dreams included either Indians or snakes — the copper colored man & the copper headed snake, then extremely common. Happily I never suffered from either (except in dread). My escape from the latter I ascribe to cowardice or, to express it more courteously, to a constitutional cautiousness beyond the existence of which my memory runneth not. This original principle of my nature, which throughout life has given me some trouble & *saved* me from some was, perhaps, augmented by two causes. 1st For a good while, I had no male companions. The sons of my uncles were too old to play with me... My cousin Osee Drake, uncle Abraham's oldest daughter, afterwards Mrs. Robert Taylor, and cousin Polly Drake, uncle Cornelius's daughter, now Mrs. Chinn, both a little older than me, were, for 4 or 5 years, my chief companions. We agreed well for they were good children and while they contributed to soften my manners and quicken my taste for female companionship, they no doubt increased my natural timidity. 2[d] My mother was, by nature and religious education, a

4 For many years Dr. Drake spent most of the vacations between his lecture courses in traveling the length and breadth of the Mississippi Valley. His journeys were for the purpose of collecting authentic information which he embodied in his monumental work, *A Systematic Treatise, Historical, Etiological, and Practical, on the Principal Diseases of the Interior Valley of North America,* the first volume of which was published in 1850, and the second in 1854.

noncombatant and throughout the whole period of her tutelage, that is, till I went from home to study medicine, sought to impress on me not to fight. Father had, constitutionally, a great amount of caution but was personally brave and, as I can now recollect, did not concur in the counsels of my mother.

At the early period of which I am writing, my health was generally good. The first illness I remember (and the only one in those days) was indeed both severe and protracted. It arose from a fall on the ice (I think) and produced an inflammation with fever on the lower part of the spine. It terminated in an abscess and an ulcer that continued for a long time. I was attended by Dr. Goforth of W. and distinctly remember how anxious I used to feel for his visits, and at the same time, how much I dreaded his probe. On the voyage down the river, he and my father had become, as the saying is, sworn friends. Father thought him on many points a very weak man, and knew that he was intemperate, but believed him a great physician. Already when 5 years old, I had been promised to him as a student and among the remembrances of that period is my being called Dr. Drake! No wonder then, as nearly 60 years have rolled away, that I sometimes have a difficulty in passing myself off for the old & primary Dr. Drake.

Soon after the settlement of Mayslick, all the people being either professors of religion in, or adherents to, the Baptist Church, a log meeting house was built about a quarter of a mile up The Road to the South and parson Wood of Washington frequently came out to preach. He was often at my father's and used to take me between his knees and talk to me on religious subjects. At length he brought with him a catechism and when I was about 6 years old and could read a little, I was put to its study. It opened with the doctrines of the Trinity which so perplexed me that I retain a prejudice against all catechisms to this hour. This parson Wood was the father of M[rs] Doctor Goforth, and I afterwards lived 4 years and a half in her family. She is now alive in Cincinnati. I often feel sorrowful that many disagreeable qualities repel me from befriending her in her old age of poverty and desolation. In her manners, she was always pleasant enough but her lack of moral principle, her ingratitude and her disposition to slander (the latter especially if indeed they can be separated) were revolting. As a wife she was extravagant and sometimes ran in debt, to a most ruinous degree.[5] Originally, she must have had many charms, for D[r] G. on the very night of his arrival at Washington, in supping at her father's table, fell in love with her, and was not long in making it known. But I must turn back...

Soon after Father settled in Mayslick, that is within a couple of years, ... a M[r] Lawson came to the same place and settled on a corner of Father's *estate!* The terms were (such as then prevailed) to build a cabin and clear as much ground as he pleased and cultivate it for five years, from the time of building, rent free. This M[r] Lawson had a son, Tom, about my own age and we were often together, a compan-

---

[5] The preceding three sentences had been crossed out of the manuscript with pen and ink of an entirely different kind from that used by Dr. Drake. With magnification, oblique and transmitted illumination, the lines were finally deciphered (see illustration facing this page).

people being either

professors of religion in, or adherents to, the Baptist Chu[rch]
a log meeting house was built, about a quarter of a mile up
the Road, to the South, and parson Wood of Washington
frequently came out to preach. He was often at my fa[ther's]
and used to take me between his knees, and talk to me
on religious subjects. At length he brought with him a ~~The~~
~~chism,~~ ~~and~~ and when I was about 6 years old and could re[ad]
a little, I was put to its study. It opened with the doctrines of
the Trinity, which so perplexed me, that I retain a prejudice against all Catechisms to this hour. This parson
was the father of Mrs. Doctor Goforth, and I afterwards liv[ed]
4 years and a half in her family. She is now alive in
Cincinnati, ~~————————————————~~
~~————————————————————————————~~
~~————————————————————————————~~
~~————————————————————————————~~
~~————————————————————————————~~
~~————————————————————————————~~
~~————————————————————————————~~
~~————————————————~~ Originally, she must have ha[d]
many charms, for D.G. on the very night of his arriv[al]
at Washington, in supping at her fathers table, fell in love
with her, and was not long in making it known. But I must
turn back.

In my letter to Echo, I mentioned Mr. Johnson of
Virginia. Soon after Father settled in Mays lick, that is
within a couple of years, a son in law of his, Mr. Lawson,
came to the same place, and settled on a corner of Father's

ionship which at length involved me in serious difficulty. I
do not recollect my age but it was six or seven. When his
father and mother were from home, he and I went into the
"truck patch" and pulled off all the young cucumbers. The
next day Tom's father made complaint to mine of the tres-
pass, and I was brought under "dealings". I remember that
father called it stealing — said it was very wicked — and that
there was danger of my being taken off to W. [Washington,
the county seat] and put in jail, a strong, dark house where I
would be all alone. The salutary impression was so strong
& durable, that I never committed another act of the kind
till after I commenced the study of medicine. (I think it was
in the summer of 1801) I was tempted early one morning, . . .
on going to feed and curry [my preceptor's] horse, to clam-
ber over the fence & get 5 or 6 peaches which grew [in the
adjoining yard] . . .

I remember another calamitous event of those days.
When about six years old, I was sent to borrow a little salt
of one of the neighbors. Salt at that time was worth about
$3 a bushel, or 12 times as much as at present. It was a small
quantity, tied up in a paper, and when I had gotten about
half way home, the paper tore, and most of the precious
grains rolled out on the ground. As I write, the anguish I
felt at the sight seems almost to be revived. I had not then
learned that spilling of salt is portentous,[6] but felt that it
was a great present affliction, and apprehended that I
should be blamed and scolded. Mother had, moreover,
taught me to consider the waste of bread or anything that
was scarce and could be used for food, as sinful. In this

[6] "It causes bad luck to spill salt."

instance she thought, I believe, that the paper had not been properly tied. When I recur to this and other incidents, which I can not definitely relate, I discover that it was an original trait of character with me, to aim at a faithful execution of whatever was confided to me and feel unhappy if, through neglect or misfortune, I made a failure. To this hour I am more solicitous about that which is intrusted to me than that which is entirely my own. Hence I have given a great deal of time to public affairs (on a small scale to be sure) but often at the expense of my private interests. "But never mind".

Another affliction becomes a matter of indistinct recollection but I had no hand in producing it. Near the same period, my father had hired a horse of a man by the name of Haines. The animal died and his owner sued father, for what sum I can not say, but one sufficient to constitute a serious calamity to the family if it had been recovered. The trial was at the county court in Washington, and gave father a great deal of trouble—mother and myself, meanwhile, at home *speculating* on the result and its consequences. Haines employed Tom Marshall...as his lawyer and father, if I recollect correctly, employed Frank Taylor... It is quite impossible that I should ever lose the remembrance of the joy in which I participated when Father returned victorious, and told mother that the jury did not leave their box (an expression which, of course, *I* did not understand) and that Marshall said that Haines was the **damnest** rascal that had ever employed him. In looking back to this incident, which occurred, I think, when I was about six years old, I find that I had a very early sympathy with my parents, and experienced sympathetic joy and grief before I could distinctly comprehend the causes of their emotions — a quality of constitution which has remained with me since I mingled in the world, and sometimes procured for me the credit of being tender hearted & benevolent from *sentiment* towards others, when I was governed by mere instinct, or "couldn't help it."

The first money I ever had, as far as I can recollect, came to me in the following manner. A man (I know not who — some acquaintance of father's) had lodged all night with us, and the next morning lost a silver knee-buckle (at that time an indispensable article) in the snow, near the door of our cabin. I was set to hunt for it, and father at length came to my assistance with a rake. I do not remember which found it, but I got the reward — a piece of cut money,[7] at that time the circulating medium of Virginia & Kentucky. My joy was unbounded; and ever since I have had it reproduced by the receipt of money. Then, it was the mere *possession* that threw me into rapture. Since I grew up, it was the idea of appropriating it to the payment of some debt that gave me pleasure. That happiness I shall, perhaps, not enjoy hereafter as much as I enjoyed it from 1806 to 1843 — through more than half my life; but I may probably find a substitute for it in some other mode of appropriation.

My first school master had the Scotch name of McQuitty, but whether he was from the "land o' cakes," I can not tell. He taught in a very small log cabin in sight of father's, up

[7] The currency of this period was mostly paper. It had a variable and uncertain value. Change was made by cutting bills (less frequently the few coins), into pieces of varying sizes, hence the term *cut money*.

the creek which flows through Mayslick; and a beautiful stream it was when it had any water running in it. My dim recollections suggest that I was about 5 years old when I was his pupil for a short time. Of my progress I can say nothing. His successor was master Wallace, whose name again suggests a Scottish origin. Under his tuition I presume I made some progress, for in 1792 and 3, I was a pretty good reader, and maintained my place respectably when we stood up to spell, before school was "let out" in the evening. My teacher then was Hiram Miram Curry, who, I think, had been a Baptist preacher & made us, I remember, "get by heart" the catechism. He taught at first in the village, south of the brook, and then up the Road beyond the meeting house, where hickory switches were abundant. I think I went to him as late as 1794, and had begun to write before I left him.

Although the country was so newly settled, at the period under review, our locality presented strange people, and novel and curious sights, almost every day. The emigration into K^y was, at that period, immense and nearly the whole passed through Mayslick.[8] Great quantities of merchandise, moreover, were hauled into the interior. My Uncle Abraham, who lived only across the Road from father's, kept both a store and tavern, at which many persons stopped. I saw aspects of things and people, which I should not have seen had we lived off the Road, and the sight of which was

---

[8] This statement is correct only with reference to the immigrants who came down the Ohio River. A greater number traveled through the *Gap* in the Cumberland Mountains and over the *Wilderness Road* in the footsteps of Daniel Boone to reach Kentucky.

no doubt intellectually beneficial. It was during this period that I first tasted wine. Some travelers from Virginia had brought it out, and the taste seems still to dwell upon my tongue. Many of the travelers were wealthy; and as the Road did not well admit of carriages, they journeyed on horseback. Thus I often saw ladies and gentlemen riding side by side, and remember I thought the latter must be the happiest persons on earth; an estimate which nearly 60 years has not entirely overruled.

(My candles both burnt out at the same moment; an emblem of the beautiful termination in old age, by death, at the same hour, of husband & wife. I have lit two others; which indicates that I am likely to keep on, though it is not far from midnight.)

From the reminiscence which I have just recorded, I find that an admiration for the sex was among the earliest sentiments developed in my moral nature. It has swayed me through life, and will, I suppose, continue to govern me to its close. When that solemn event shall come, I hope to see female faces round my bed,

> And wish a woman's hand to close
> My lids in death, and say — *Repose!*

As years rolled on, Father began to conclude (very justly) that he should aim at a larger farm, seeing that the cultivation of the soil was his destiny, and that he had two sons and two daughters. Uncle Abraham Drake, moreover, was anxious to own the little tract on which father resided, as it so immediately adjoined his own. He had purchased 200 acres of one Shannon, lying about a mile directly West of Mayslick, and offered to exchange it for the place on which father resided. A bargain was at length concluded, and the deed is now in my possession. It is dated, I think, in the summer of 1794, when I was in my 9th year, and your uncle Benjamin (I believe, though perhaps incorrectly) an infant at the breast.

This was a new era in my life. The land acquired was covered with an unbroken forest, which must be cleared away, and a new cabin erected. Father was still too poor to hire a labourer for steady work, and was, himself, far from being a robust and vigorous man. My health was good and my spirit willing—I might, therefore, render some assistance in his new enterprise; and accordingly master Curry's hickory and myself parted, never to meet again. I was provided with a small axe—father had a larger, and a mattock for grubbing. Thus equipped, with some bread & meat wrapped in a towel, we charged upon the beautiful blue ash and buckeye grove, in the midst of which he proposed to erect his cabin.

Many days, however, did not pass away before each received a wound! Of the two, father's was the most honorable. Getting his mattock fast under the roots of a grub, and making an effort to disengage it, in which he stooped far forward, it suddenly came out, and he brought, by a jerk, the axe extremity of the implement against his forehead, making a gash through to the bone. Mine, which did not happen on the same day, was made by a jack knife, which passed more rapidly through a crust of bread than I expected, and made a deep wound across the ball of my left hand,

the scar from which remained till it was obliterated by my
great burn, 34 years afterwards.[9] The loss of blood was not
sufficient in either case to arrest the march of improvement
and, day by day, we made new conquests over all that stood
in our way. Shrubs and bushes were grubbed up; trees
under a foot were cut down, and those of a larger diameter
"girdled," except such as would make good logs for the
projected cabin, or could be easily mauled into rails. It was
father's business, of course, to do the "heavy chopping";
mine, to "hack" down saplings, and cut off the limbs of trees
and pile them into brush heaps. The forest consisted chiefly
of blue ash — tall, straight, soft while green, easily hewed &
easily split into rails and puncheons; of sugar trees — generally preserved; of several kinds of hickory and walnut, and
of Buckeye. The last was so soft that it soon became my
favourite, and to the readiness with which it yielded to my
axe I may ascribe the affection which I have ever since
cherished for it.[10] I loved it in proportion to the facility with
which I could destroy it. But its obliging temper was not
limited to *my* demands. It had a parasite, which sought the
air and light of heaven by climbing to its limbs, and weaving

[9] On the evening of September 28, 1828, the bed of Dr. Drake's sister-
in-law, Miss Caroline Sisson, caught fire after she had retired. He rushed
into her room and succeeded in checking the flames by compressing the
burning bed covers with his naked hands, which were severely burned.
Miss Sisson succumbed eight hours after the accident. It was several months
before Dr. Drake recovered, and his hands were badly scarred.

[10] At the 45th anniversary celebration of the founding of Cincinnati held
on Dec. 26, 1833, Dr. Drake in his response to a toast extolled the virtues
of the Buckeye and wove the history of the Ohio valley into his speech. He
suggested that this was a suitable emblematic tree for the state, with the
result that ever since then Ohio has been termed *The Buckeye State*.

those of many adjoining trees into a broad and tangled canopy. That parasite was the winter grapevine.

The brush was of course burnt up as fast as it was cut, and of all the labours in the forest, I consider that of dragging and burning the limbs of trees the most delightful. To me it made toil a pleasure. The rapid disappearance of what was thrown upon the fire gave the feeling of progress—the flame was cheering—the crackling sound imparted anima- tion—the columns of smoke wound their way upwards, in graceful curves, among the tall green trees left standing; and the limbs & twigs of the hickory sent forth a balmy and aromatic odor, which did not smell of the school house.

In due time a "log rolling" frolic was gotten up, when the buckeye showed that, if pressed too far, it could resist; for its consumption by fire was affected with more difficulty than that of any other tree. The ground being prepared, and the logs collected and hewed on one side, the new cabin, a considerable improvement on the old, was "raised" and brought to some degree of finish; though glass could not be afforded, and a kitchen could not be put up till a stable had been first built. At length the day for removal arrived, and we left the village and public roadside, with its cavalcade of travelers, for the loneliness of the woods; a solitude which very soon was deeply felt by us all, but most of all, I think, by mother. Thence forth for 6 years I passed a happy life of diversified labour; but as it is now after 1 o'c'k A.M., I shall reserve the events of that period for some other time, and perhaps some other correspondent.

Your affectionate   Father

MAIZE FROM SEED TO
BUCKEYE BOWL

THE SETTING

Doctor Drake was not only fond of Alexander Hamilton McGuffey but he had a high regard for his scholarship, as is clearly
shown in the following letter with its numerous allusions to
authors and books. Although consisting primarily of a description and use of Indian corn, Drake, consciously or otherwise, is
stimulated into disclosing his own broad scholarship.

It is extremely interesting that the opinion of the literary world
concerning the merits of the *Rambler* as compared to the
Spectator would seem to be, at the present time, in agreement
with Doctor Drake.

Letter Three

MAIZE FROM SEED TO BUCKEYE BOWL

To Alexander Hamilton McGuffey [1]

Louisville [Kentucky]
Saturday P.M., Decr 18th, 1847.

My dear Son:

Twelve hours ago, I finished a letter of 18 pages to your brother, Charles, which I shall send off tomorrow. It was preceded by one to your sister, Echo, of 15 pages which must have reached her this morning. At the end of each, I determined to write no more this winter on the same subject, but here I am already violating my good resolution. Well! I must confess my weakness and go ahead. You are, yourself, in part to blame for having urged me so often to write down some recollections of my early life. While thus engaged, I am, of course, not writing on my book which I am sure you will regret. But do not fear that the spirits of

---

[1] Alexander Hamilton McGuffey (1816-1896), lawyer and author, married the elder daughter of Doctor Drake, Elizabeth Mansfield, in 1839. Although the entire credit for the popular McGuffey readers is usually given to William Holmes McGuffey (1800-1873), his younger brother, Alexander, was the author of two: McGuffey's *Eclectic Spelling Book* (1837-8) and McGuffey's *Rhetorical Guide* (1844) which later became the *Fifth Reader*.

the shadowy past will frighten off the stern realities of the present and make my lectures as dreamy as my letters. On the contrary, as far and well as I myself can judge, I have never lectured with greater force and fluency than through-out the present week. In fact, an excited state of feeling is a great help to the mind, at least to mine; and although I was wide awake till after two last night, communing with the boys of a buried generation, I found no difficulty this morn-ing in lecturing to the youth of the present living age on the nature and diagnosis of chronic pleurisy.

Although I am now, in continuation of the labours of the past night, commencing a letter to you, I expect at 7 o'c'k to lecture with exuberant sound and gesture before the Physiological Temperance Society[2] on the diseases pro-duced by habits of daily drinking. Some minds are equally tense, and vibrate in the same tone, whenever or however struck. Others, like the fiddlestring, must be screwed up and brought into tension, before they will send forth intel-lectual music. Mine belongs to the latter class, and requires the stimulus of lively emotion to rouse it into activity. My pupils, then, are not likely to suffer by my fit of auto-biographical *furor,* however much I may suffer in the estimation of my children by the garniture of vanity and egotism in which I walk before them. It is related of some great man that while romping & riding on his cane with his

---

[2] The Physiological Temperance Society of the Louisville Medical Insti-tute (later University of Louisville, School of Medicine) was organized by Dr. Drake in 1841. He was not a total "abstinenter." Instead, he served punch from a buckeye bowl in his own home. However, Dr. Drake con-stantly advocated *moderation* with reference to "ardent spirits" i.e. rum, whiskey, brandy etc.

Alexander Hamilton McGuffey with daughter Anna

little children, a young friend entered the parlor, to whom he said: "Don't tell any one what you have seen till you become a father." In like manner I say, don't tell any one of my displays till you arrive at the age of sixty-two, and begin to connect the past, instead of the future, with the present.

(When I finished the preceding word, I laid down my pen, as the sun had gone down, to call at the post office for the 3^d time today; but the mail which should have arrived at 10 last night is not yet in. How artistical we have become since my boyhood! At that time a river flood with a rapid current, would have greatly facilitated the transmission by water of a mail from C. to L. but now it impedes it. The current was the natural power — steam has supplanted it.)

The close of my letter to Charles found Father's family log cabin denizens of the wilderness a second time, and myself, the oldest child, 9 years of age. To make you acquainted with the character of the influences under which I was now placed, and was to remain for the next six years (when I departed for C. [Cincinnati]), it is necessary for me to dwell on the condition of things around us.

When we arrived at Mr May's deer lick, in the autumn of 1788, there were no inhabitants in that part of the county. But immigration, like that of the Western Reserve when you were an infant, was a constant, not a mere wet weather stream. Within the six years that elapsed, the number of settlers had increased to such an extent that one could not wander a mile in any direction, without meeting with a clearing of two to ten acres, often enclosed with a brush fence, and designated as a human residence by a one story unhewed log cabin, with the latch string always out. The usual number of ragged children [was] around the door, or playing in warm weather, under the shade of some shellbark hickory or venerable sugar tree, which might perchance have escaped the axe of the destroyer. By the way, it is remarkable that it should have remained for De Tocqueville, at a very late period, to pronounce an eulogy on the power of that noble instrument, without which the forests of the West could never have been sub- dued and made the abode of civilized man. An axe weighed from 3 to 4½ lbs. avoirdupois, according to the strength of him who was to wield it. The helve was invariably made of shellbark hickory, of an ovate shape, about two feet four inches in length, and having always scratched upon it a one & two feet measure for the purpose of measuring off the "rail cuts" or the cabin logs. Grindstones were scarce, but every house was provided with a whetstone, and when the instrument was newly sharpened, woe be to the boys or the women who might dull it against a stone or turn its edge by cutting the bone of a gammon of bacon. The lower part of the helve was always made smaller than the upper, so as to give it a slight degree of elasticity which not only increased the power of the instrument, but saved the hand from a jar in using it. Finally, it was a rule, never to be violated, to warm the blade or edge in winter before pro- ceeding to chop hard wood; otherwise it might break. To this moment it is wonderful to me that so many different things could be done with this simple instrument—that it could be made to perform the functions of so many others

—and that a single man in a single day could, by its aid alone, destroy so many trees.

(I wonder, also, if it isn't time for me to go the meeting of the Society at the University? Yes! My watch says 25' past 6 o'c'k so, for the present, you will be let off.)

9 P. M. Well, I have just got back to my chair and writing table, but to get back to the same point in my narrative may not be so easy. When we first went into the woods and I was sent out to hunt up the cow, I used to break the bushes as I strolled along and if I did not find her, they would guide me back; if I did, I had but to follow in her unerring steps. In my abrupt and rapid sally from the path along which I was leading you, I broke no bushes, and, if following her should not restore me to [the] point at which I left you, I know not when we shall meet again.

In Cincinnati & Louisville we think of the cow in connection with our tea & coffee, our butter, custards & ice creams; but we never see her. We are like thirsty people drinking from the impure & sluggish stream long after it has left the rocky fountain. In your native Western Reserve the cow is thought of as a source of wealth, and valued as so much trading capital. Far different was her rank and condition in the early times of which I write; for old Brindle was then a veritable member of the family, and took her slop at the cabin door, while the children feasted on her warm milk within. The calf grew up in their companionship, and disputed with them for its portion of the delicious beverage which she distilled from the cane and luxuriant herbage

[45]

in which she waded through the day. It was my function when our rival was likely to get beyond its share, to take it by the ears and hold it away till mother should get ahead; and many a tough struggle did I have. I spoke just now of slop, but Brindle had other food at milking time. From October till January the pumpkin was no unimportant part of her diet, and nothing could afford richer and sweeter milk.

In the absence of every kind of cultivated fruit for pies, the pumpkin, moreover, was a resort of inestimable value, and hence it was among the staples of every little field of overshadowing corn, acquiring a vast size and delicious flavour in the fresh calcareous soils, and was gathered in when the corn was pulled. Abounding in saccharine matter, its juice, boiled down, made a very tolerable molasses, in the manufacture of which I worked many a day with my mother for the few first years after we entered our forest home. It was also "cut & dried" for spring.

To prepare the new field for cultivation required only the axe & mattock, but the cultivation itself called for the plow & hoe, both of which I recollect were abundantly rude and simple in their construction. Deep plowing was not as necessary as in soils long cultivated, and if demanded would have been impracticable, for the ground was full of roots. After a first "breaking up" with the coultered plow, the shovel plow was in general use. In such rooty soils it was often difficult to hold the plow and drive the horse. It was the employment of small boys, therefore, to ride and guide the animal — a function which I performed in plowing time for many years; and it was, I can assure you, no sinecure. To sit bare-back on a lean & lazy horse for several successive hours, under a broiling sun, and every now and then, when you were gazing at a pretty bird, or listening to its notes, or watching the frolic of a couple of squirrels on the neighbouring trees, to have the plow suddenly brought to a dead halt by running under a root, and the top of the long hames to give you a hard and unlooked for punch in the pit of the stomach, is no laughing matter, try it who may! One of the severest I ever had was rendered more calamitous from contrasting my situation with what it was but an hour before when Father, finding it impossible to manage both the horse and the plow, in a piece of ground that had just been cleared, came and took me to the field from a little log school house a quarter of a mile off where I, with other boys, was idling away my time under the sway of master Beadle; of whom I may possibly say a word hereafter.

For several years our chief article of cultivation was Indian corn, but near the center of the field, in some spot not easily found by trespassers, was a "truck patch"; in which water melons and musk melons were planted, while in some corner we had a turnip patch. If the former supplied the place of peaches in the season for that delicious fruit, the latter were a substitute for apples throughout the winter. The virgin soil of Kentucky produced the best turnips that ever grew: at least, such my recollection would make them, after the lapse of 54 or 5 years. The tubers literally rested on the ground and only sent their spindle shaped roots into the loose black mold below. In December, when at night the family were seated (father and mother on split bottomed turners chairs, and the children on stools) around a warm fire, made blazing bright with pieces of hickory bark, a substitute for candles, and every member was engaged with a dull case knife in scraping and eating a sweet and juicy turnip, the far-famed pears and apples of their native Jersey were forgotten by the "old people." The perils and privations which followed on their arrival were remembered only to be rehearsed to their children who knowing of no higher enjoyment than that in which they reveled, had nothing to wish for more. Yet, more was within their reach. Several luxuries from the surrounding woods were, on other evenings, substituted for that which much more deserves the name of *pomme de terre*, than does the potato. These luxuries were walnuts, hickory nuts, and winter grapes, so called because they were too sour to be eaten till they had been sweetened by several severe frosts. To lay in a store of the two former delicacies was my special duty when the walnut & hickory drop their fruit among the fallen leaves but the climbing vine often required father's axe to bring its lofty *fulcrum* to the ground. Your Latin lore will enable you to apprehend the meaning of this technical term which you will please explain to Dove and Echo & Margaret and Belle, adding in apology for me, that my Botany has been so long neglected that even *it*, not less than walnut gathering, has become a reminiscence and claims its place in the family circle of resuscitated thoughts.

But I must reconduct you to the corn field, the scene of my earliest labours and most cherished recollections. Nothing is equal to the Indian corn for the settlers of a new and isolated spot. At the present time when steamboats not only transport the movers to every point, but afterwards supply them with flour and every needful article of food, the value of corn to the first settlers of Kentucky can only be estimated by those who witnessed the pressure of the arm of civilization against the resisting forest, and saw that men had to support themselves while they were performing the very labours from which support must come. In the new soil, corn, with moderate cultivation, yielded from 60 to 80 bushels to the acre. Every domestic animal fed and flourished on it—the horse, the cow, the sheep, the hog and the dog who, as wheat bread came into use, would not eat it. The blades of corn up to the ears were "pulled" as the latter began to harden and when partly dry were tied, with blades, into bundles; the tops above the ears were cut off and shocked. After the corn was pulled, [the tops] were hauled in and covered the long fodder house, in which the blades and husks were stowed away while the corn was measured and thrown into a crib of long round poles. Here then were provender and provision for the coming winter. Neither wheat, nor rye, nor barley, nor the far famed potato could have been substituted for the admirable maize.

Several things in its cultivation can be done by small boys, and from my 8th year, I participated in them. When the field was cross furrowed, the furrows being about 4 feet apart, dropping the corn was a simple task, and father, following with the hoe, would cover it. When I was a little older and the furrows ran in one direction only, much greater skill was requisite; for the rows must be kept straight and parallel, that cross plowing might be practiced.

The method then was, as it still is, to cross the furrows at right angles, in lines four feet apart, by the aid of stakes or sharpened poles, generally of hickory or pawpaw, with the bark peeled off, so as to be white and easily seen. To drop by the range of these stakes had something in it that was intellectual or scientific, though I knew not then that there were such terms. It was, at least, more difficult than the other mode; and I should not at this time feel prouder to describe it graphically than I then was to perform it with speed and accuracy. (It's after 1 o'c'k: I'm in the Sabbath—so good night!)

Monday 11 P.M. -20th—Although the evening is far spent, I take up my pen to put down a few more corn field reminiscences. I fear you will get tired of the corn field, as I sometimes did myself, notwithstanding my relish for its labours compared with some others. As soon as the young corn began to "come up" two most acute and active animals began to pull it up. They were crows and squirrels; in both of which the surrounding woods abounded. The crows would light on any part of the field, the squirrels attacked the outside rows; for the old lady's plan of having no outside rows which President Polk has borrowed without acknowledgement, in his scheme of having no national frontiers, had not been invented. It was my special function to repel these aggressions. To this very hour I continue to wonder at the instinct which enabled them to know that grains of corn were attached to the young shoots. My means of defense were very harmless and may almost be summed up in the word, *noise*. Old Lion, however, was a faithful ally and I made a *show* of resistance with clubs and stones. The enemy never made battle but always retreated with notes of bird or beast contempt for my power, and from the top of some neighbouring tree looked down in defiance till I passed on, when they would quietly descend and recommence their feast. To the corn field hollowing of those days, I may, perhaps ascribe the strength of lungs & larynx which, after the lapse of 55 years, enables me to lecture longer & louder than any of my colleagues; although, with one exception,[3] they are so much younger.

In the progress of time, however, I began to raise a noise of a different kind, which silenced the note of contempt and, now and then, secured to me a very different triumph from that of making the enemy fly or run away. When I was about 11 years old, father purchased me a little old shot gun, and I circum-perambulated the little field with the eye of a hunter — and the self importance of a sentinel on the ramparts of a fortress. My trophies for awhile were, like those in the practice of medicine 11 years afterwards, neither numerous nor brilliant; but the enemy felt my power, and lost much of his audacity. Old Lion comprehended the whole matter and would look into the tree when I was about to fire. When a squirrel is wounded, he often falls to the ground and runs for some other tree. Then was the moment for my faithful ally, and to him in many instances I had, in justice, to ascribe an equal participation in the victory. This

[3] Charles Caldwell, M. D. (1772-1853), Professor of the Institutes of Medicine and Medical Jurisprudence in the University of Louisville. He was the author of an unusual autobiography, published posthumously, of which Sir William Osler said: "Pickled, as it is, in vinegar, the work is sure to survive."

same good old Lion (I call him old because it is a familiar epithet but in fact he was very junior) and myself were boon companions and co-workers. When the hogs got into the corn field he would labour till the last was lugged out. If mother wanted a chicken he would run it down and hold, without biting it, under his paws. When I went into the woods he would "tree" squirrels for me; & when I was out after dark he kept by my side, and taking one of my wrists in his mouth would run with me till I got out of breath. And this service, still, it would be ungrateful in me to forget.

All the neighbours, of course, kept dogs & being naturally **timmid,** when I was sent on an errand (which in those days meant borrowing or bringing home something you had lent), I was often afraid, when I went alone, to approach the cabin, but when Old Lion went with me I was as brave as a lion. It was then that I first learned how rapidly courage rises when we discover that the danger is falling. Expressed mathematically, courage is inversely as the danger. To this very hour I am afraid of many things, and, among the rest, that you are tired of the scenes and scenery of the corn field; still I must keep you in it a few minutes longer, although it is *"past 12 o'c'k"* (as the watch-man is now proclaiming with a voice loud enough to drive away a flock of crows).

By the month of August the corn is in silk, and the air becomes redolent with the peculiar odor of the tassels. The young and milky grains then begin to form, and then the crows and squirrels recommence their depredations, and the labour of watching is, or rather was, renewed. Now approached the daily feast of green corn — the era of "roasting ears," which began as soon as the grains were half grown, and continued until no more milk would flow out on piercing the integument with the thumb nail. Such a field, at that time, was the children's paradise. My first business in the morning was to pull, and husk & silk enough for breakfast; and, eaten with new milk, what breakfast could be more delicious? In the latter part of summer and in early autumn, after the corn was "laid by," various rank weeds, including Spanish needles and wild-cucumber vines, covered with an armature of bristles, would spring up among it, rendering the "pulling" and hauling in, a most uncomfortable work. Once I got a bristle in one of my eyes and came near losing the sight. Always we returned from the field at night black with Spanish needles (Bidens [[4]] of the botanists as I learned 10 years afterwards).

In hauling in the corn one fall, I got hurt a little and began to cry. Two men were assisting father and myself, one of whom was my cousin, Jacob Drake. They laughed at me, which made me cry the harder, whereupon they laughed still louder, and I, bent upon alarming them or awakening their sympathy, bawled at the top of my voice; but producing no effect, had to give up the contest and go to work. I do not recollect that I have ever made any decided effort to excite the sympathy of others since that time though I have always had a puerile taste and itching for it. At the same time, I must say in justice to myself (for a

---

[4] *Bidens bipinnata,* L. Dr. Drake, in his early medical career, was an enthusiastic botanist, and his first professorship was that of Materia Medica and Medical Botany (1817) in Transylvania University, Lexington, Ky.

man must be just to himself not less than to others) that I have a constitutional tendency to sympathize with others (which I do not confound with the sentiment of benevolence). From this trait of character, I suppose, I was much taken with Adam Smith's Theory of Moral Sentiments when I read that work nearly 40 years ago, though I have no doubt that it embraces some fundamental errors. We come now to the "husking" but as I have grown quite too sentimental for such a scene of rivalry and nocturnal uproar and as it is, moreover, 1 o'c'k A.M., I will bid you *Good Night.*

Tuesday 21ˢᵗ Decʳ P. M. Although the corn husking frolic was always at night, it turns out my description will be written in the day. The fact is, that having lectured and made some business calls, I am seated at my table and must go at *something*. Dʳ Johnson in the Rambler, or some other moralist in some other book, has said, that in labours of the intellect, we should always go at the one to which, at the time, we feel the strongest inclination, for we shall not then perform any other as well as that. Speaking of the Rambler, which I used to read when a young man, leads me to say that I preferred its style to that of the Spectator — yet the literary world has decided differently. This proves that my own taste in style was not good. But, perhaps, the weight and depth of thought in the former, decidedly greater, it now seems to me (from *recollection,* for I no longer find time to read either) than in the latter, gave me a relish for its style. Howbeit, I have probably a natural taste for balanced periods, in which the words present antithesis and the ideas antagonism.

But I must pass on to the antagonisms of the cornhusk-ing. When the crop was drawn in, the ears were heaped into a long pile or rick, a night fixed on, and the neighbours notified, rather than invited, for it was an affair of mutual assistance. As they assembled at nightfall the green glass, quart whisky-bottle, stopped with a cob, was handed to every one, man and boy, as they arrived, to take a drink. A sufficient number to constitute a sort of quorum having arrived, two men, or more commonly two boys, constituted themselves or were, by acclamation, declared captains. They paced the rick and estimated its contractions and expansions with the eye, till they were able to fix on the spot on which the end of the dividing rail should be. The choice depended on the tossing of a chip, one side of which had been spit upon. The first choice of men was decided in the same manner and in a few minutes the rick was charged upon by the rival forces. As others arrived, as soon as the owner had given each the bottle, he fell in, according to the end that he belonged to. The captains planted them-selves on each side of the rail, sustained by their most active operatives. There at the beginning was the great contest, for it was lawful to cause the rail to slide or fall toward your own end, shortening it and lengthening the other.

Before I was 12 years old, I had stood many times near the rail, either as captain or private, and although 50 years have rolled away, I have never seen a more anxious rivalry nor a fiercer struggle. It was there that I first learned that competition is the mother of cheating, falsehood and broils. Corn might be thrown over unhusked, the rail might be

pulled toward you by the hand dexterously applied underneath, your feet might push corn to the other side of the
rail, your husked corn might be thrown so short a distance
as to bury up the projecting base of the pile on the other
side. If charged with any of these tricks, you of course
denied it, and there the matter sometimes rested — at other
times the charge was re-affirmed, then rebutted with "you're
a liar," and then a fight, at the moment or at the end, settled
the question of veracity. The heap cut in two, the parties
turned their backs upon each other, and making their hands
keep time with a peculiar sort of time, the chorus of voices
on a still night might be heard a mile. The oft replenished
whisky bottle meanwhile circulated freely, and at the close
the victorious captain, mounted on the shoulders of some
of the stoutest men, with the bottle in one hand and his
hat in the other, was carried in triumph around the van-
quished party amidst shouts of victory which rent the air.

Then came the supper on which the women had been
busily employed and which always included a "pot-pie."
Either before or after eating the fighting took place & by
midnight the sober were found assisting the drunken home.
Such was one of my autumnal schools, from the age of 9 to
15 years.

And now, I suppose, you hope I am done with Indian
corn, but not so, I am only done with the field and the
frolic. Its preparation for the table must not be overlooked!
I mean preparing it for the hands of the cook. A reference
to the manufacture of meal excites my imagination as much

as the "meal-tub plot"[5] excited that of our English fore-fathers, though peradventure, the excitement is of a very different kind. I am struck with the contrast between the simple machinery of those early times and the present complicated and effective flouring mills of the same region and over the West generally; many of which are impelled by steam, although when I first participated in the meal manufacture there was not a steam engine in the United States.

Our first and cheapest implement was the tin grater 8 or 9 inches long. It was used to reduce to a sort of pulp the unripe corn when it had got too old for roasting ears and was too soft to pound or grind. The ear was rubbed up and down on this instrument over which, at the age of 7 or 8 and still later, I often tired my right arm and sometimes lacerated my fingers. When the corn had got ripe and dry, it was sometimes thrown into the hominy block and sometimes taken to the hand mill. The concavity or mortar of the block was made by burning. The pestle was an iron wedge (used for splitting rails) let into a wooden handle. Many a long hour did I toil over this mortar—which, for aught I know, was one cause why I was averse to the study of medicine. As this was not the mortar Shakespeare had in his eye, I can not (classically) lay the blame of my cramped genius upon it, and still I must be indulged in the opinion that its power in developing the mind is not equal to its efficacy in developing the muscles of the arms.

[5] The papers outlining the plot of the Duke of Monmouth (1649-1685), illegitimate son of Charles II and Lucy Walters, were reputedly kept in a meal tub.

Mary **Wolstoncraft**[6] remarks of girls that were compelled to sew a great deal, in her day, as a part of their education, that their ideas at length came to follow their needles. In like manner mine went up and down with the pestle. The needle made progress but the pestle, like a paper dancer between two electrified plates, still continued to move up and down, forever up & down! Time, however, which cures almost everything except egotism and garrulity, so applied his skill to my feelings against the hominy block, that 45 years afterwards when I saw, at Mackinaw, two Chippewa squaws pounding their corn in the same mortar (in the manner of the two Jewish women), I felt no repugnance at the sight.

To the wedge and mortar succeeded the hand mill. A rod with its upper end run through a hole in a board, and its lower resting in a cavity or hollow, pecked out near the circumference of the upper millstone, was seized with the right hand, while the left threw the corn into the large opening at the center. Here again was motion without progression; but the meal flowed out and its stream was augmented as the velocity of the stone increased, giving to the effort *immediate* reward which, down to the present hour, I have observed to be the greatest stimulus. My Father

---

[6] Mary Wollstonecraft Godwin (1759-1787), beautiful English authoress and early champion "of the rights of women." Extremely liberal, if not libertine, in her views, she was first associated with Captain Gilbert Imlay, an American writer then in France, by whom she had a daughter. When this alliance terminated, she cohabited with William Godwin (1756-1836), English author, whom she later married. Their only child, Mary, held the same liberal views as her parents, associated with Percy Bysshe Shelley and, after the death of his first wife, was married to him.

never owned a hand mill, but on those of his neighbours, when 10 or 12 years of age, I have ground many a small grist, often taking my sister Elizabeth to lend a hand to the work. We, of course, went on foot and I "toted" the peck of corn on my back.

9 P.M. Water and horse mills had been built before I was old enough to perform the labours I have just noted but they were, for many years, few and feeble. The former, built on the smaller streams, could be run only in wet weather, and even then a part of the water had to be employed in sawing boards, of which none could be received from abroad. The latter required two horses to turn them, and were greatly thronged, as were the water mills. When a bag of corn, always ranging from 2 to 3 bushels, was taken, 9 times out of 10, it was necessary to leave it and wait till its turn came. My Uncle Abraham Drake built two mills on Lee's creek, a little north of Mayslick, and when I was 9 years old, I was taken to them by Father. Having learned the path which lay through the woods, I was soon intrusted with the whole duty except that of putting on and taking off the bag to which, of course, my strength was not adequate. But skill as well as strength was demanded, for if an equal division of the corn was not effected, the lighter end would soon begin to rise & the lower to sink. I had many anxious trials of that kind. The only resource was to stop by the side of a stump or log, on which I could stand, throw up the heavy end, restore the nominal balance and remount

from the same spot—endeavouring afterwards to sit most on the light side. My constitutional caution did me good service on these occasions. Had my bag at any time fallen off, I could have done nothing but cry over it, till some wayfaring man or stouter mill boy might, perchance, come that way. When I visited Mayslick in 1845, nearly half a century afterwards, I found certain spots on the mill path which bore the aspect of old acquaintances, and certain trees which I greeted as old friends.

Among the horse mills to which I used to go, was one three miles off, built by Mr. Polk, perhaps of the same family with the president. The first time in my life that I undertook to sit up all night was at his mill. I became so sleepy that the very recollection of it makes me think of laying down my pen and "retiring" but I must not do so till I tell you that we sometimes went 10 & even 12 miles to horse and water mills; the former at Flemingsburg & the latter on Licking River. These were fine opportunities for seeing the world; and it was on one of these lazy, listless rides, the horse always merely walking, that I first noticed the influence of soils on the character of the forest. We passed suddenly out of the woods of the rich lands on which we lived (the diversified—*Arbustum terra fertilis*) into a forest of white oak, supported by an argillaceous soil. Such lessons, I now perceive, are not without their beneficial influence on a young mind. Why may we not as well read them in the book of nature as in Virgil? Is it not as well, or even better, to see a landscape than its picture?

The distant water mill of which I have spoken, was two

miles above the Blue Licks[7], so noted in latter years as a watering place. It was then famous for its salt. Eight hundred gallons of water had to be boiled down to obtain a bushel! Father's mode of paying for it was by taking corn or hay; for the region round about it produced neither. It was my privilege first to accompany him when I was about 11 years old. By that time he had got a small meadow. He took as much hay as two horses could draw, and after traversing a rugged and hilly road, bartered it for a bushel of salt.

The trip was instructive and deeply interesting. I again passed through a zone of oak land and when three miles from the springs, we came to an open country, the surface of which presented nothing but moss covered rocks interspersed with red cedars. Not a single house or any work of art broke the solemn grandeur of the scene, and the impression it made was **indellible.** I here first observed the connection between rocks and evergreens, and have never seen it since without recurring to this first and wildest sight—even now a bright vision of the mind. Thus I had

---

[7] A celebrated watering place in Kentucky during the first half of the nineteenth century. In its vicinity, there are still traces of the trails of the buffalo and other wild beasts which came from great distances to "lick" the earth because of its saline content. This was also the scene of one of the bloodiest conflicts of the Revolution between Kentucky pioneers and a superior force of British and Indians who had continued hostilities long after the war's cessation in the Atlantic states. This engagement is referred to as "the last battle of the Revolution" because it was fought on August 19, 1782, almost a year after the surrender of Lord Cornwallis at Yorktown. Part of the battlefield is now the site of a state park in which there is a commemorative monument and a museum of antiquities.

seen three varieties of the earth's surface and three modifi-
cations of its natural productions. I had tasted the salt
water, seen the rude evaporating furnaces & smelt the salt
& sulphurous vapour which arose in columns from them.
I had learned that immense herds of buffalo had, before the
settlement of the country, frequented the spot, destroyed
the shrubs and herbage around, trodden up the ground and
prepared it for being washed away by the rains until the
rocks were left bare. Finally, I was told that around the
licks, sunk in the mud, there had been found the bones of
animals much larger than buffalo or any other known in the
country. Thus my knowledge of zoology was extended and I
received a first lesson in geology . . . I could tell my mother
& sisters of strange sights which they had never seen.

Those sights, and others which I now and then saw,
gave, I believe, a decided impulse to the love of nature
implanted in the heart of every child and to them I ascribe,
in part, that taste which at the age of 60 rendered my travels
for professional inquiry into new regions of the diversified
and boundless West, a feast at which I never cloyed. Had
I, at that time, been incarcerated within the walls of an
Academy conjugating Latin verbs or learning Greek alpha
betas, I might possibly have became a man of some erudition but lost, perhaps, that love of nature which has been
to me throughout life an exhaustless source of enjoyment.
This, at least, is a harmless, perhaps even a praiseworthy
speculation, for it is certainly commendable to submit
gracefully to our deprivations, and sophistry cannot be
condemned when employed to reconcile us to conditions
that are irremediable.

Well, I believe we have at last disposed of the corn. No, we have neglected the shelling. That which is now done by machinery was then done with the hand, and often did it raise blisters on mine over the soft cushion in front of the first phalanx of the right thumb. This shelling was the work of nights or rainy days. In winter a sheet or coverlet was laid on the middle of the floor and all the children old enough to hold an ear were set to work. A part of the cobs kept up the blaze of the fire while the others were laid up into houses by the children too young to shell; father meanwhile quietly smoking a cob pipe in the corner. As it is now after 11 P.M., I haven't the heart to try your patience further, so—*Good night.*

Thursday Night, Dec 30*th*. In consequence of Dr. Yandell's sick head, I lectured at his hour[8] this afternoon having, of course, filled my own at 11 A.M. As I wish to make my letter a new year's messenger ("gift" I will not venture to call it, and "present," it can not be dubbed, as it relates to the *past*), I must bring it to a close tonight and mail it in the morning. And now the momentous question comes up, shall I send it off with its present *limited limits* or extend them to what may be called a respectable length, say 30 pages? The decision, I shall, as the judges say, keep in reserve.

I have dwelt so fondly on the cultivation of corn that I begin to fear you will think my life and labours as a farmer

[8] Lunsford Pitts Yandell, Sr., M.D. (1805-1878), Professor of Chemistry and Pharmacy in the Medical Department of the University of Louisville.

were restricted to that vegetable (equivalent to regarding me as a boy of *one* idea). I must, therefore, show you that I "lent a hand" to some other farming work.

The *new* soils of Kentucky were not good for wheat and the weavel, moreover, in "them" days (to speak in the dialect of the field) "done" great injury to that grain. Father & mother, however, like the other immigrants, longed for wheat bread and, as soon as practicable, wheat was sown. The fallow was but little attended to and the sowing was generally in the cornfield, sometime after the corn had been "laid by." The ground had to be plowed with the shovel plow and until I was 12 years old it was my function to ride the horse & have both legs stuck with Spanish needles up to my knees. Having no shoes & stockings (superfluous things in early autumn) & tow trousers, which would slip half way to the knee, the service was not the most enviable. After about my 12th year I was able to hold the plow & guide the horse. A narrow wooden harrow or a brushy limb of a tree and subsequently the hoe covered up the grain and finished the rude "seeding."

Harvest was a social labour, a frolic, a scene of excitement and, therefore, a much more desirable era than that of seeding. My first labour in that field was to carry the sheaves to the places on which they were to be shocked. The next was to bind up the handfuls of cut wheat, a more difficult task for a small boy. My ambition was to wield the sickle. The maxim of the harvest field was that no boy becomes a good reaper till he cuts his left hand. Notwithstanding my characteristic cautiousness, I cut mine several times, and have this moment looked at a long scar on my little finger (more honorable in my *own* estimation than if made by a Mexican sabre) which has stood me as a remembrancer more than half a century. If I should ever become so rich and vain as to mount a diamond ring, it will remind me of the days when I would have reaped a week to get enough money to buy a "pinchbeck" ring for my good sister Lizy. When I was 13, 14 & 15 years old, I was able to do "half a man's" work with the sickle and I may add (boastingly) with the scythe also, in our little meadow.

As I have already intimated, harvest was a kind of frolic. Several hands were generally collected and the whisky bottle circulated freely. On such occasions, mother always had a "time on't" for there must be many extras on the table. I often had to leave the field and give her some assistance for Lizy was her only help. Pigs, calves & sheep or some of them were sacrificed to the occasion.

One harvest was characterized by an event which exerted on me a permanent influence. Father had a ram that well understood my **timmed** character and scarcely ever failed to make at me when, if I had no stick, I took to my heels. One day I was going over the pasture where he was with a butcher knife in my hand (for what purpose I do not recollect) and coming near him, he as usual, made at me. Thus armed, I determined to stand my ground. He dodged the knife with his head as he gave the butt and it entered the side of his neck and bled him to death! Having acted in self defense, my scolding was not a very serious affair; but the next day, when some of the mutton was served up to the harvest hands in a potpie, it inspired me with disgust, from which I have not yet recovered.

In the harvest field my greatest ambition was to sweat so as to wet my shirt. I then first noticed that, under the same circumstances, men sweat more than boys; but the circumstances were not precisely the same for the former drank more whiskey than the latter and it contributed to the sudorific effect. I was, however, more sparing than many other boys for I well recollect that the conduct of men who were "fuddled," as it was jocularly called, was disgusting to me and while yet a small boy I was a "temperance man" though not always a total *abstinenter*. Many of my harvest field contemporaries have long since descended into a drunkard's grave. How thankful I ought to be to Him from whom cometh every good and perfect gift that I have been preserved from that inglorious & revolting fate.

The "harvest home" was not a frolic. Father & I generally performed the work ourselves. We had no barn or mow, and both wheat & hay were stacked out. I soon learned the art of building stacks and was the architect while father did the heavier work of "pitching up." I could now build a very respectable stack of either wheat or hay—I mean one that would turn off the rain and be so balanced as not to be blown over by the winds. The interest I took in this engineering is to this moment a pleasant reminiscence. [It] brings up another to which you must permit me to make reference.

Before I was 12 years old I could do nothing about fencing but haul the rails. This was done by placing the log chain round the ends of six or eight and then driving the old horse to the place they were wanted. I was too small to lay them up and before I got large enough for such lifting, I undertook to lay the worm, that is, the ground rail. This was done by setting up two rows of stakes parallel to each other and five feet apart, then taking a grubbing hoe and marking the ground, keeping in the range of two stakes. Thus there were parallel rows of checks and the ends of the "pannels" of fence were brought out to them. As I got older the hoe was dispensed with and I "sighted" by the stakes as I laid the ground rails down. It is quite impossible ever to forget the self importance I felt when I first found myself employed in this practical geometry and father and a hired man laying up the rails after me.

When I was on the old farm in the spring of 1845, I went to the spot of my first achievement. The slope and jutting rocks were there but no vestige of living nature remained. Even the great honey locust stump which had stood in my way had decayed and disappeared. Thus men and animals and trees — all that have life — yield to the destroyer while the mineral features of the earth remain almost unchanged. The fig trees of Judea are no more, but the natural cavern from which the Saviour called forth Lazarus was, it is said, lately visited by Harriet Martineau![9] The temple of Solo-

---

[9] Harriet Martineau (1802-1876), English writer and traveler. Her *Retrospect of Western Travel* (London, 3 vols.; New York, 2 vols., 1838) which describes her journey through the United States in 1834 is one of the best and sanest of the American travel diaries. In Cincinnati she was entertained by Dr. Drake and his daughter who took her for a "delightful drive, the pleasure of which was much enhanced by his interesting conversation . . ." Later at the tea-table set in Dr. Drake's garden: "I doubted whether I had ever heard more sense and eloquence at any old world tea-table than we were entertained with as the twilight drew on." She quotes at length from one of Dr. Drake's addresses relative to the West (London ed., vol. II: 226-231; New York ed., Vol. II: 41-44).

mon has crumbled into dust but Lebanon, which supplied the cedars which adorned it, still rises in unaltered grandeur. With these evidences before us of the certain destruction of everything which has life, how cheering and glorious is the hope that He who said: "Lazarus, come forth" will, in His own time, call on all who trust Him to leave the tomb and be with Him.

I have spoken of mowing and must return to the meadow while I say that Father was in the habit of leaving a corner uncut that the timothy might go to seed. When I was about 12 years old, a patch was left for my special benefit. When the seed was gathered and winnowed, father and I proceeded with it to the "Lick" (as the village was by abbreviation called) where it was bartered for a sufficient amount of "fustian" to make me a "round about" and a pair of pantaloons with something else (I don't recollect but believe it was cheap Marseilles) for an "under-jacket." This was my first "boughten suit." I fear that when I made my appearance at the "meeting house" the first sabbath that I put it on, my thoughts were not much better than they will be when I visit St. Paul's[10] in the new suit of broadcloth you are to send me down.

The transition from the meadow to the "flax patch" is easy for a fence only separated them. The pulling, threshing, spreading out to rot, taking up & stacking flax were works which no one need to covet. Many a long day through many a year I had my hands made sore by them. Other manipulations were postponed till winter. It was then dried

[10] St. Paul's Episcopal Church which, at that time, was located on 6th Street between Green and Walnut Streets, Louisville, Ky.

over a slow fire, sunk below the surface of the ground, and "broke," a very hard work for a boy but one which I performed through many a tedious day. The "swingling" was better fitted for boys and constituted the only thing in the cultivation & preparation of flax in which I took pleasure. It required skill and, although it tired the right arm, it did not demand the strength which the "break" required. It covered one (moreover) with tow & shives (an evidence of effect) and at night the flax could be weighed which gave interest to the labour. I have often observed, as I walked the streets of Cincinnati, how much the wood sawyers, when working together, talk about their work. I recollect how much my mind then dwelt on the quantity I should "swingle" by night. If I had been wielding the swingling knife to day instead of lecturing twice and tonight writing down the exploits of days in which my hair was as flaxen as the dressed bark of the *Linum usitatissimum* of Egypt, would I not have been as happy? Multiplication of ideas does not necessarily bring increase of happiness.

Among the labours of the latter 3 years of my country life was that of mauling rails. This was generally done in winter, and, although a most laborious work, I took delight in it and still recollect it with pleasure. A *green blue*-ash was my choice, for it was easy to chop and easy to split; but I often had to encounter a dead honey locust in the field, which was a very different affair. When I was 14 I could "cut & split" 75 rails a day out of the former and from 40 to 50 out of the latter. Still I was not large for my age; but was inured to labour, and (why I cannot explain) was willing to pursue it either alone or with father. When I got a tough log the wedges & "gluts" would fly out on being struck a hard blow. Gentle taps were necessary to get them well entered. I have often observed since that many failures occur, in the enterprises of human life, from want of patience in giving the gentle taps which are necessary in beginning them. I have profited by this in my letters. The first,[11] to Dove, was of 12 pages only — this covers 32! and, I am almost tempted to enter on another sheet!! However, I'll be considerate & subscribe myself your

Affectionate Father.

---

[11] Although written first, this letter which describes his preparation in 1799-1800 for the study of medicine, is No. X, page 235.

FARM ANIMALS AND
"SUGARING OFF"

THE SETTING

At times Drake's early training in an uneducated group is quite apparent. For example, he may use an objective, instead of the nominative, personal pronoun: "Old Lion and me sometimes took a little hunt . . ." [the *me* has been partly rubbed out and an *I* substituted]. For such slips as this, his apparent method of effacing was either to use a piece of cloth (possibly his handkerchief) or the end of a finger which had been moistened. (At this time the germ theory of disease was embryonic.) When he desired to obliterate a passage more completely, he used his pen and made slanting strokes criss-cross through the words.

Occasionally Dr. Drake slips in spelling. However, the reactionary purists of syntax will be happy to observe that he rarely splits an infinitive.

Letter Four

FARM ANIMALS AND
"SUGARING OFF"

To James Parker Campbell[1]

Louisville, [Kentucky]
Decr 31st, 1847 — ½ past 9 P.M.

My Dear Son,

When I look at the date I have just written down, I think it highly probable that this is the last letter I shall begin before the year 1848, and equally probable that its end will be in that year.

This morning I sent off an epistle covering 32 pages to brother Aleck; which I mention that you may not be alarmed; for *after* such an effort, a long letter is not, you know, very likely to be brought forth, for want of materials and want of strength if they existed. In said letter, I detailed the most important of my labours as a farmer's son from the

---

[1] James Parker Campbell (1806-1849), husband of Dr. Drake's younger daughter, Harriet Echo. He was a native of Pennsylvania, emigrated to Chillicothe, Ohio, and then to Cincinnati, after his marriage, June 4, 1839. He was a packer of pickled pork and similar products. An exemplary man, he worked incessantly in fitting up a temporary hospital during the 1849 cholera epidemic in Cincinnati. He contracted the disease and succumbed within less than twenty-four hours.

age of 9 to 15 years. In this letter I shall resume the wandering narrative, and prosecute it, I expect, in a still more desultory manner. I shall most likely say less of crops and more of stock; which will perhaps suit your taste, as merchants deal more or less in the stocks, have stock in trade, and sometimes trade in stock until they lose their stock in trade. As the weather is warm, wet, & *thundery*, I hope your stock of hogs is not great at this time; and should it be, I trust you will stand stock still in your slaughtering operations; for I well recollect that in former times, cold & dry weather was desired at "killing time."

Jan. 1ˢᵗ Saturday afternoon. I need not tell you that when I wrote the foregoing page last night, I was as stupid as a *stock*. This morning my 3ᵈ & last lecture on Pulmonary Consumption roused me for a little while—how I now am, I cannot tell, it remains to be seen.

From the age of 8 to 15 I had much care of our stock; for boys can do that kind of work. The cows & sheep had to be hunted up in the woods, & driven home at night, one of each dignified with a bell. That of the sheep always on a higher & shriller note, which with the deeper & graver tones of the cow bell still lingers in my ear. On hearing a cow bell in the woods, you can tell whether the animal is feeding or walking (towards home for example). In the former case the sounds have no observance of time, will be suspended for many seconds or almost a minute, and then the clapper will strike once or twice or several times. In the latter case there is a regular rhythm, an according with time, for the ringing is produced by the walking.

When our sheep laid out in the woods, they were often destroyed by the wolves, which still infested that part of the country when I left it for the study of medicine. Father's cabin stood on a side hill, and was not **underpined.** The lower end was three feet from the ground, and here was the winter shelter of the sheep—furnishing security from both wolves & weather. Still, although there was protection from rain and snow, the cold wind was not excluded, and it often became necessary for me to bring the young lambs into the cabin above & let them spend the night near the fire. The exercise of this kind office towards the young & suffering innocents was, perhaps, one cause of my repugnance to eating their flesh for many years afterwards. Sometimes they would lose their dams, and then it would become necessary to feed them on cow's milk—a labour which generally fell to me, and I used to hold their mouths in the buckeye bowl till they *learned* to drink.

In the latter part of winter we were often short of fodder for our stock, and had to resort to the woods with both cattle and horses for *browse.* Of the whole forest, the red or slippery elm was the best, next to that the white elm and then the pignut or white hickory. It was then that I first observed that the buds of these & other trees grow & swell during the winter, a fact which interested me much. Ten years afterwards, when Darwin's Botanic Garden fell into my hands, I took the deepest interest in that part of the poem (the 2ᵈ) which is entitled "Economy of Vegetation."[2] Two lines which come up in my recollection, seemed to me the very soul of poetry. They are:

"Where dwell my vegetable realms benumbed,
In *buds* imprisoned or in bulbs **entoomed**."

The critics have condemned that poem, & neither you nor any for whom this letter is intended have ever read it or ever will; & yet it afforded me great pleasure. If you should chance to stumble on a copy of it, pray purchase it for me. To my cow-boy labours when 12 or 13 years old, for hours together in the woods around our little fields, in the month of February, I ascribe in part my admiration of that poem. It still awakens in me delightful romantic recollections of that distant period.

[In winter], my equipments were a substantial suit of butternut-linsey, a wool hat, a pair of mittens, and a pair of old stocking legs drawn down, like **gaithers,** over the tops of my shoes to keep out the snow which was quite as deep in those days as in later times and a *great deal prettier.* (Don't smile, *if* you please, till you hear me out). I do not mean that

2 Erasmus Darwin, M.D. (1731-1802), English physician and botanist, and grandfather of Charles Darwin. Dr. Drake has slipped again. Part I contains *The Economy of Vegetation* while Part II treats of *The Loves of the Plants with Philosophical Notes.* The quotation is from Part I, Canto I, lines 459-460, (page 44 of the 1791 London edition):

"Where dwell my vegetative realms benumb'd,
In buds imprison'd, or in bulbs intomb'd."

Although Byron said: "Pompous rhyme — the scenery is its sole recommendation," it was greatly admired by many of Darwin's contemporaries.

the separate flakes were more beautiful than at present; but that *a snow* in the woods of those days was far more picturesque than a snow in or around town as we see it now.

The woods immediately beyond our fields were unmutilated and not thinned out as you see them at present. They were, in fact, as nature received them from the hand of her Creator. When a snow had fallen without wind, the upper surface of every bough bent gracefully under its weight, and contrasted beautifully with the dark and rugged bark beneath: — the half decayed logs had their deformities covered up; the ground was overspread with a covering as pure and white as the souls of Nelly or Anna or Mary or Etta[3] (sweet darlings, how I want to kiss them!). The cane as high as my head and shoulders, with its long green leaves made the *alto relievo* of the snowy carpet: — the winter grapes hung in what seemed *rich* clusters, from the limbs of many trees, which were decorated with tufts of green mistletoe, embellished with berries as white as pearls; while the *Celastrus Scandens* [Climbing Bitter-sweet], a climbing vine hung out from others, its bunches of orange red berries; and the Indian Arrow wood (*Euonymus Carolinensis*) [E. Americanus, L., Strawberry Bush] below, displayed its scarlet seeds suspended by threads of the same colour.

With axes on our shoulders, father and I (sometimes one only) were often seen driving the cattle and horses before us to the nearest woods, and when the first tree fell, the browsing commenced. As the slippery elm was soft and mucilaginous, twigs of considerable size were eaten, and

3 Grandchildren.

the bark of larger ones stripped off. Other trees being chopped down, we occupied ourselves, more or less, in cutting wood for fuel or timber for rails. But the time required for browsing was not always devoted to work, for the tracks of "coons" & rabbits had *attractions,* especially to myself and old Lion, and I often had opportunities for gratifying the instinct of man and dog for hunting.

In winter, rural economy at nightfall is, in a new country, before barns and stables & sheds have been built, an interesting period of the day. The stock must be collected, fed and disposed of in the best manner possible for the night. Did you ever pass an evening under such circumstances? The memory of such evening scenes can never fall out of my mind. The voice of the hungry and impatient calf still rings in my ears. As the evening approached its cry was sent forth, and the tones, slightly tinged with the mournful, to this hour, when I chance to hear them repeated, awaken in my heart a kind of romantic melancholy.

Father & Mother were early risers, and I was drilled into the same habit before I was 10 years old. In winter we were generally up before the dawn of day. After making a fire, the first thing was feeding and foddering the horses, hogs, sheep & cattle. Corn husks, blades & tops had to be distributed, & times without number, I have done this by the light of the moon reflected on the snow. This done at an earlier hour than common, old Lion and I sometimes took a little hunt in the woods; but were never very successful. I had a taste for hunting, but neither time nor genius for any great achievement in that way. Among the pleasant recollections of those mornings are the red birds, robins and snow birds, which made their appearance to pick up the scattering grains of corn where the cattle had been fed. I well remember my anxiety to get some fresh salt to throw on their tails. I often made conical lattice traps, and set them; but not, I believe, with any great tact, for my captures were not numerous.

Our stock required attention in other seasons of the year than the winter. For several years our fences were low & open, and the corn field was a place of irresistible attractions. The horses & sheep would jump the fence, the cows would throw it down with their horns, and the hogs would creep between the rails—when the cry would be, "Run, Dannel! Run!" and away went Dannel with his fellow labourer, old Lion.

It was a custom with father and some of his neighbours in those days, to take their mares and colts & the horses which were not yet broke into what they called the *range*. Within 3 miles of where we lived, on Johnson's fork of Licking, there were no settlements, and consequently, there was a luxuriant herbage consisting largely of what was named pea vine, with a full growth of Buffalo grass. The months of May, June & July were selected for this resort to the untrodden wilderness. Some salt was tied up in a rag (for paper was scarcer than the raw materials), and when we reached a wild and unfrequented spot where there was water, the salt was placed on the ground to be licked up. From this "whetter of the appetite" the animals eagerly fell on the rich herbage, which they devoured with as much avidity as I feasted my eyes on the surrounding scenery; which from its being "oak land" presented many productions and aspects different from the woods with which I was more familiar. When the horses had wandered off a little way we left them; and it is remarkable that they would remain there, and make the spot where they were salted a kind of rallying point or place of resort.

Another summer & autumnal labour, which may be called a "joint stock" concern, for it included both horses & cattle, was driving them (when kept in the field) to the "pond" for drink. At that time (as I believe it still is), the neighbourhood of Mayslick was very deficient in stock water through the months of August, September and October. But just beyond the western boundary of Father's little farm, a short mile (if there be such) from where we lived, there was a permanent circular pond of clear, cold water, covered with a small green floating plant called *Lemma* by the Botanists. To this pond it was my evening duty to drive the cattle and horses; and from it we sometimes had to haul water, in a whiskey barrel, on a log sled. This water was for washing, but mother, from various causes, was not always supplied, and sometimes the washing was done at the pond. On such occasions I was an important personage, as I helped to carry the clothes, kept up the fire, and dipped up the water. From some distance round the neighbours frequently went there to wash, and thus it happened, now and then, that there was a little party there, and a good deal of social chit-chat. This pond was the only water in those parts deep enough for the boys to bathe in and it was resorted to for that purpose. It might have been taken for one of the sources of the "Styx" from the quantity of sunken brush it contained; and was, moreover, prolific in water snakes and mud turtles. Nevertheless, with all my characteristic timidity, I was often in it. I recollect *(when father was from home)* to have left my work on a hot day, and, running the whole distance, plunged into this cold pool without experiencing any injury.

Our spring, as you will believe from what has been said, was of the wet weather variety. During the long **drougths** which now and then happened, it either afforded an insufficient supply for cooking & drinking or went, as the saying was, "dry." During such periods, water for ordinary use had to be brought (not from the pond, which was unfit) but from a permanent spring half a mile distant where, as a tenant, lived an old Leather Stocking by the name of Rector, of whom more hereafter. Of course I was the chief water carrier, though Sister Lizy sometimes accompanied me. To this hour I could lay down the path, partly through a field and partly through the woods, which I so often traveled for that purpose, 50 and 53 years ago. The common method was to *"tote"* a small bucket on my head, at which, if I were not equal to the old negro women in the neighbourhood, I became quite a "dabster." By the way, Mrs. Hentz,[4] in her late work — *Aunt Patty's Scrap-bag* has drawn a faithful and graphic picture of the wenches in the South balancing buckets of water on their heads without touching them with their hands. This, I must say in justice to myself, I could do in those days of ample practice.

About two-thirds of the way from father's, there lived in

[4] Mrs. Caroline Lee (Whiting) Hentz (1800-1856), popular, though mediocre, contributor of both prose and verse to the periodicals of her day in the United States. *Aunt Patty's Scrap-bag* was first published in 1846.

the edge of the woods in a very small log cabin, a widow, Mrs. Day who had seen better *days*, with a daughter Katy, a little older than myself, and a son, Morgan, a little younger, where I sometimes stopped and loitered away my time; for, at that early period, my social propensities were as great as at present. I know not where Katy is, but in 1844, when at Lexington, Missouri, I found my old play mate, Morgan, looking older than myself and still bigger. He had for many years been intemperate, but, when I was there, was reformed & sober, and took much interest in promoting the delivery by me of two or three temperance lectures. This was (by water) 1000 miles further in the West, than the woods in which his mother's cabin stood. In the country around Lexington, I saw much display of the state of Society in which we passed our boy-hood. The frontier had indeed advanced a thousand miles in about half a century; and we unexpectedly met upon it, when both had got on the "Western side of the hill of life." The meeting brought up many reminiscences, from which I derived (as I thought) more pleasure than he experienced; which I ascribed to my having taken more pains to cherish my early recollections.

I must return to the horses. The next year after Father moved to the woods, a traveller came along one evening on a mare, with a young and tired colt following him. He wished to get rid of it, and proposed to father to take it. The proposal was agreed to, the traveller kept on to Mayslick, and the colt was declared to be mine. This was my first article of property — my last possession of the same kind was the mare which I gave your wife. I have forgotten *her* name, but I remember that I called my filly *Tib*. My devotion to

Page 12 of Letter IV, illustrating Dr. Drake's method of erasure

her was of the most laudable kind, but she proved to be a weakly orphan, and never became more than a tolerable pony. Of course she was as gentle and almost as domestic as old Lion; keeping round the door among the children with whom she maintained a kind of companionship. Her hair became as long & shaggy as that of a buffalo. When she was two years old, she could bear my weight, and one of my amusements was to lock my feet under her body, turn her head towards the spring and make her trot down the hill. When she was four years old, father's necessities for an abler horse led him one day...to swap her off, and by giving some boot, to get an abler horse. To this hour I feel dissatisfied with myself for having so willingly parted with poor *Tib*. But it is, perhaps, some excuse to say that I had got to be something of a horseman and like other equestrians was ambitious to make more of a figure than when mounted on the back of the '*Pet*,' as we often familiarly called her. Thus it is if we rise faster in the world than our early friends, we are ever disposed to part company with them.

Fond of horses, I should perhaps, have become an expert, and for one of cautious temperament an adventurous horseman, but for an event which came nigh destroying my life. I was about 11 years old when father placed me on a young horse, which was supposed to be tolerably well "broken." He and another man were walking near me up the lane, and presently I found them lifting me up from the hard road. I had been thrown by the animal over his head so suddenly that I was never able to recollect the fact. Being very seriously injured, I was ever afterwards "afeard" of wild and wicked horses.

Throughout the period of which I write, Father aimed at raising horses for sale; and one of them proved to be very fine. Not satisfied with any price offered him at home, Father resolved to try a *foreign* market, & it was no other than the *adjoining* county of Bourbon. There he sold him to M^r — afterwards Col. Garrard, a son of old Governor Garrard. In part pay, he took a hundred gallons of whisky. When it arrived we felt quite rich. A barrel was immediately tapped, and the "tin quart" scoured bright as possible, and put in requisition. Our customers were of course the neighbours, most of whom regarded it a duty to their families and visitors, not less than themselves, to keep the whiskey bottle well replenished. For a friend to call and find it empty was a real mortification to one party, and quite a disappointment to the other who was apt to revenge himself by speaking of the matter to some other neighbour as an instance of mean-ness, or (more accurately) of stinginess.

There were some families in the neighbourhood how-ever, who did not keep nor drink whiskey. They were Methodists, and it was a rule in the Methodist Church, at that time, that its members should not drink ardent spirits. They were, in fact, the first Temperance society after the Rechabites.[5] They were reproached, however, for their total abstinence, and I recollect to have heard father say that he had "no doubt they drank behind the door." Yet he himself,

---

[5] There appears only one reference to the Rechabites in the Bible, Jere-miah: XXXV: 5-19. The Rechabite movement was apparently one to stem the tide of luxury and license among the Israelites. These sons of Rechab led a simple nomadic life, refused to drink wine, scorned agriculture and planted no vineyards.

a professor of Religion, always drank temperately, and should have spoken differently.

The sale of the whiskey devolved largely on me. I had learned, moreover, to write a little, and mother made a small blank book in which I charged most that I measured out. Thus I was once a sort of bar keeper or, at least, commenced my mercantile career by retailing whiskey. At 7 this evening in the midst of the letter in which I am recording this early history, I had to lay down my pen, and deliver in the University before our Physiological Temperance Society a lecture on the diseases produced by excessive drinking. I took care not to tell the audience that I was once engaged in selling whiskey to a whole neighbourhood, and felt very glad when I saw a boy coming with his junk bottle or half gallon jug. The price was "eighteen pence" — 25 cents — a quart.[6] The price of a yard of coarse India muslin in those days was from one & six pence to two shillings; that of a bushel of corn from 9 pence to one and thrippence! Pork was from a dollar and a half to two dollars. One other article comes into my mind. I assisted father in pulling a small wagon load of turnips. We drove 9 miles to Washington, and bartered them at 9 pence a bushel for "store goods."

I must not forget to tell you that I was once an assistant

[6] At the close of the Revolution the predominant currency in the Confederation was that of Great Britain, though Spanish dollars and certain of the French coins were in circulation. In July, 1785, Congress adopted the dollar with a decimal ratio as the unit of money but it was not until April 2, 1792 that an act creating a coinage system was passed. However, for many years thereafter, the monetary system was unstable and, at times, became chaotic.

manufacturer of charcoal, which seemed to me at that time quite a dignified employment. I assisted in chopping & stacking up the wood, and the wonders of the coal pit made a very strong impression on my imagination, as the peculiar odor of its smoke, escaping through the earth which covered it, did on my senses. I can almost smell it as I sit here, writing about it after the lapse of (that everlasting) 51 or 2 years.

Speaking of the coal pit reminds me of the wood pile. This was composed of green & dry logs, dragged from the woods or fields on a log sled. Father generally did the chopping and I the hauling. To chop it 4 or 5 feet long for the fireplace after it was drawn near the door was commonly my labour; and I took good care to perform it on the spur of the occasion only; that it is never to have any great stock ahead. I often had to cut off a large "back log" in a cold winter morning, before a fire could be made; and sometimes to do the same thing when the rain was pouring down. We never seemed to have thought of the great advantage of a shed to secure, at all times, a supply of dry wood, or of the equal convenience of a *pile* of wood ready cut and split.

Now, I suppose you are as tired as I often was before I got through a dry honey locust log, yet (although the watchman has cried "past 12 o'c'k!") I can not let you off till you have made an excursion to the sugar camp. There were but few sugar trees on Father's land, and he rented a "camp," as the grove was called, about two miles off. Our tapping was with the axe. The troughs were rudely dug out with the same tool & generally of Buckeye, as being a soft wood which, moreover, was not apt to crack during the summer.

One or two iron kettles, with the old iron pot, were swung over a log fire, before which was a kind of half faced camp covered with clapboards, as a shelter from the rain. While father did the wood chopping and kept up the fires, it was my province to drive "old grey" with an open barrel on a sled, turning and winding through the woods, to collect the sugar water. Sometimes we staid *all* night, but generally got home before morning. In the best sugar weather the water ran only in the day, and when the flow had not been very great, we would bring the sugar with us. When it had, the "graining" had to be postponed to the next day. The work was one of great fatigue and exposure, but I recollect it with unmingled pleasure; for it was something out of the ordinary course of labour — it was *sweetened* with abundance of rich syrup. We took milk along, and made spicewood tea with the syrup — the time was that in which many trees and shrubs had begun to unfold their buds — the birds had begun to chirp and **carrol** — the leaves of the cane were green — the wild **turkies** occasionally paid us a visit — and to top out the whole, we were laying in a good supply of sugar for the coming year — and, I should add, of molasses, too. After this detail, you will not be surprised that my reminiscences of these scenes and labours are so *sweet;* and that, to this hour, I prefer maple sugar and maple molasses to any others.

Well, now I'll let you off; and promising not very soon again to **compell** you to travel through 17 pages of an old mans boying recollections, subscribe myself, as ever

Your affectionate Father

PRIMITIVE ARTS AND CRAFTS

THE SETTING

Dr. Drake, in this letter, emphasizes the illiteracy of his parents to which exception has been taken (*see* Note No. 4 in Letter One). The description of their accomplishments shows that both his father and mother were remarkably well versed in rural arts. His mother seems to have been not only an excellent disciplinarian but a true *mother* in all the finer connotations of that word. She was also a careful housekeeper and unusually skilled in the diversified crafts required in rural economy.

Letter Five

PRIMITIVE ARTS AND CRAFTS

To Margaret Austin Cross Drake[1]

Louisville, [Kentucky]
Jan[y] 7th, 1848 — Friday 4 P.M.

My Dear Daughter,

After my lecture this morning, I was detained in my university-room, by students who desired medical advice, at the end of which time, it being one o'c'k, I started home and having to pass the door of our Reverend friend, M[r] Breckinridge,[2] I concluded to stop and "take a cup of tea." There I met with D[r] Todd[3] of Danville, who spent the winter with me in Phil[a] 42 years ago, and in the spring, descended the river with D[r] **Farrer**,[4] D[r] Richardson[5] and

---

[1] Margaret Austin Cross Drake (1812-1896) second wife of Charles Daniel Drake.

[2] Rev. William Louis Breckinridge, D.D. (1803-1876) member of a prominent early Kentucky family and the pastor of the Second Presbyterian Church, Louisville, from 1836 to 1858.

[3] John Todd, M.D., a graduate of the Medical Department of the University of Pennsylvania in 1810, a trustee of Centre College, Danville, Ky., from 1833 to 1841, a second cousin by blood and an uncle by marriage of Mrs. Abraham (Mary Todd) Lincoln.

[4] Bernard Gaines Farrar, Sr. (1784-1849) began the practice of medicine in 1807 at St. Louis, Mo., where he became widely known as a physician and surgeon. He was the first president of the Missouri Medical Society. In 1820, he married Ann Clark Thruston, niece of both General

myself. Many long years have rolled away since I saw him last, and of course our minds turned instinctively upon "lang syne."

All this is but an introduction to what I now announce, (viz¹)—that to my having this morning lectured on Dyspepsia, you may ascribe my commencing, at this time, the reminiscent epistle which I am about to write, in continuation of the series in which I find myself (most *unpremeditatedly*) engaged. Now for the proof: My lecture on Dyspepsia was the moving cause of my having so many dyspeptics and hypochondriacs to visit me—the examination of their cases detained me till dinner time—that caused me to stop at Mʳ B.—that brought me into company with Dʳ Todd — that brought up old recollections, and *they* prompted me to set at this letter without delay. Behold, then, a regular (catenation or) linking of cause and effect! How strikingly this illustrates those arrangements of Providence which set all our prescience at defiance. But, in further illustration, I find that I am likely to go off on a different path from what I intended, and will, therefore, as I used to do in boyhood, when I had taken the wrong road— cut across the woods to the right. Well! I am now at it, and will move forward. But as I travel it, and fancy *you* by my

---

George Rogers Clark (1752-1818), early immigrant to Kentucky, builder and commander of the first blockhouse at the Falls of the Ohio (Louisville, Ky.) and of Governor William Clark (1770-1838) of the Lewis and Clark expedition, and territorial governor of Missouri from 1813 to 1821.

5 William H. Richardson, M.D. (died 1845), friend, admirer and associate of Doctor Drake in the Medical Department of Transylvania University, Lexington, Ky., in 1817-1818 and from 1823 to 1827. Dr. Richardson was Professor of Obstetrics, Diseases of Women and Children.

Margaret, wife of Charles Daniel Drake

side (which always delights me)—to what objects shall I direct your attention? Indeed, I can not say myself; but we must *start*, for until we do, nothing can be seen.

In my last two letters to Alex & James, I gave some account of those outdoor labours which exerted on my constitution and character effects which, as well as I can judge, have continued to the present time. I might have extended that account much further without exhausting my stock of recollections; but chose to limit myself to such an amount as would illustrate the influence on my character of rural occupations & events. In close connection with them were numerous domestic labours & incidents, and to them I will devote a few pages (*more* or less).

Up to the time of my leaving home at the age of 15, my mother never had a "hired girl" except in sickness; and father never purchased a slave for two substantial reasons: *first*, he had not the means; & *second*, was so opposed to slavery that he would not have accepted the best negro in Kentucky, as a gift, provided he would have been compelled to keep him as a slave. Now & then, he hired one, male or female, by the day, from some neighbouring master (white hirelings being scarce), but he or mother never failed to give something to the slave in return for the service. In this destitution of domestic help, and with from 3 to 6 children, of which I was the oldest, you will readily perceive that she had urgent daily & nightly need of all the assistance I could give her. To this service, I suppose, I was *naturally* well adapted; for I do not now recollect that it was ever repugnant to my feelings. At all events, I acquiesced in it as a matter of duty—a thing of course—for what could she do — how get on — without my aid? I do not think, however, that I reasoned upon it like a moralist, but merely followed the promptings of those filial instincts of obedience, duty and cooperation which are among the elements of a system of moral philosophy.

P.M., ½ past 9. When I had written the preceding pages I broke off for supper, and then attended a Friday evening devotional meeting of communicants of our church, from which I have just returned; for after the exercises were finished, I remained half an hour for conversation. By this meeting a new train of thought and feeling has been raised in my mind, and I can scarcely place myself on the spot we occupied, when I parted from you.

The readiness to join my mother in the daily performance of her various and often tiresome duties, of which I was speaking, had in it the less merit, inasmuch as there was little to attract me from them. In and around our cabin, from the door of which we looked into the woods on every side, there could not be much of evil companionship. How often we are virtuous merely because there are no present motives to vice. Nevertheless, on the main, as I can now recollect, I performed my labours *con amore;* always, however, all things being equal, I preferring those of the field with father.

I have already spoken of grating and pounding corn, toting water from a distant spring, holding the calf by the ears at milking time, going to the pond on wash days, and divers other labours with which mother was intimately connected. But my domestic occupations were far more extensive than these. To chop, split and bring in wood; keep up the fire, pick up chips in the corn basket for kindlings in the morning, and for light, through the long winter evenings when "taller" was too scarce to afford sufficient candles, and "fat" so necessary for cooking, that the boat-lamp, stuck into one of the logs of the cabin over the hearth, could not always be supplied, were regular labours. To bring water from the spring, which was but a short distance from the house, was another. To slop the cows, and, when wild, drive them into a corner of the fence, and stand over them with a stick while mother milked them, was another. Occasionally I assisted her in milking, but sister Lizy was taught that accomplishment as early as possible, seeing that it was held by the whole neighbourhood to be quite too "gaalish" for a boy to milk; and mother, quite as much as myself, would have been mortified, if any neighbouring boy or man had caught me at it.

In 1842, when I was sailing on the Northern Lakes in quest of information on the condition, customs, and diseases of the Indians, a gentleman, who had been much among them told me that as he was once traveling a bridle path, he saw some distance ahead, an Indian family about to meet him. The man had on his shoulder a heavy pack, and his wife was following him. They instantly stepped aside into the woods, and when they resumed the path, the burden was on *her* shoulders. It is evident that he had some tenderness of heart, and while they were alone he was willing to relieve her, & she willing that he should do it; but neither could consent to his performing so feminine a labour in the sight of others. The rifle was his appropriate burden. Thus it is, from the bark wigwam to the log cabin, & thence to the palace, public opinion displays its fantastic tyrannies! By a strange inconsistency, while it proscribed milking by boys, it permitted churning. If I had as many dollars as times I have lifted the "dasher" I might give up teaching, and devote the remainder of my days to writing nonsense for the amusement of my grandchildren. If I could have as many rational wishes gratified as I uttered wishes that the butter "would come," I should have nothing *more* to wish for in this life. But, in truth, like pounding corn into *meal,* in a hominy block, it was a hard and monotonous employment, especially in the latter stages of the process, when the butter rises on the "dasher."

Friday was mother's wash day, and then, when the duties of the field were not urgent, I left it for the house. A long trough dug out of the trunk of a tree stood under the back eaves to catch rain water for washing, and during times of drought, when a shower came "up," all the wash tubs & buckets of the house were set out. Still, it often happened, that much had to be brought from the spring and "broke" with ashes. Mother's rule was to begin early and finish by noon. My additional duties were, to keep up the fire, take care of the children, and assist in hanging out the clothes, which, for want of line was often done on the fences. To bring them in at night, when they were generally frozen in winter, was still more my business.

Scrubbing & scouring were generally done on Saturday, and to the former I often lent a "helping hand." Till I went to Cincinnati to study medicine, I had never seen a scrubbing *brush.* We always used a "split" broom, in the manu-

facture of which I have worked many a rainy day & winter
night. A small hickory sapling was the raw material. The
"splits" were stripped up with a jack-knife and the right
thumb, for 8 or 10 inches, bent back & held down with the
left hand. When the "heart" was reached and the wood
became too brittle to strip, it was cut or sawed off, & the
"splits" turned forward, and tied with a tow string made for
the purpose on the spot. It only remained then to reduce the
pole above to the size of a handle.

A lighter and genteeler work was making "scrubs" for
the Buckeye bowls, and the good old black walnut table
(bless it!) with a crack in the middle, from end to end,
occasioned by the shrinking of the boards. The "*Scrub*" was
a short hand broom made precisely like the "scrubbing
broom" but out of a smaller sapling. If I were not afraid you
would think me boastful, I would say that when 12 years
old, I was decidedly dexterous in the manufacture and *use*
of both—though I generally had rather a poor "Barlow"
knife—price eighteen pence—with which to execute the
former. Peace to thy name, good M*r* Barlow! Thy ingenuity
used to excite my wonder! Thou wert present with me in
many a useful labour; and, while at work in thy shop in
London,[6] thou wert my companion in many a romantic
ramble through the woods beneath which *Absalom*[7] rolled
his spring water over the limestone rocks.

Our most important manufacture (I mean mother's &

[6] The 'Barlow," a one-bladed jackknife has been the favorite of many
generations of boys. The first recorded English cutler of the name was
Edward Barlow who was elected a *Master Cutler* in 1653.

[7] A small creek near Mayslick, Mason County, Ky.

mine) was soap making. Father constructed the "ash-hopper" which was composed of clapboards, arranged in an inverted pyramid. In the bottom was thrown some husks, or straw, or dry buffalo gross, to act as a strainer. It was filled with ashes, on the broad surface of which the water was, from time to time, poured by the bucketful. A trough beneath received the ley which, over a fire in the yard, was boiled down till it was "strong" enough to float an egg. The fat was then added & the boiling continued till the soap "came." By the aid of salt, we sometimes made an imperfect hard soap, to be used for special purposes. It was in making soap that I got a scald just above my left knee, the smooth scar from which still remains, and would serve to identify me with "Dannel Drake" if it should be necessary.

When speaking of milk and butter I forgot to tell you that I knew the art and mystery of cheese making, often prepared the rennet, and assisted in squeezing out the whey from the curds. Although Father made the press, I was mother's "right hand" man in managing the long lever, while she placed the cheese beneath its fulcrum.

December was our "killing time." I shall not take you to the hog pen, nor the scalding tub, but begin with cutting up the fat, a work to which boys are well adapted. The fat being "tried" out, the next labour was "chopping" sausage meat, which I began with a hatchet because too small to lift a heavier tool & continued till I could use the axe with a vigorous arm. The stuffing, twisting into links, hanging on poles, and moderate smoke drying succeeded. Lastly, the frying & the *feast,* for in those days of simple fare, the annual return of the sausage season was hailed by the whole family. To this hour I prefer good & especially *clean* sausage to any other meat.

The same season & the same killing were followed by other labours of an interesting kind. A Jersey house keeper could never neglect or forget the delicious mince pie, in the manufacture of which I have wielded the "chopping axe" full many an hour. For a long time, however, apples were too "dear" and scarce to justify a large application to that object. Our compositions, compared with those of modern times, were abundantly simple, but on that account more salubrious, and as our tastes were formed to no more savory mixture, they were eaten as delicious.

Other dainties still awaited us as the result of killing hogs. They were "dough-nuts" & "wonders"—the latter being known to you under the name of "crullers." I can find neither word in Webster, and from early association, prefer the former. These sweet compounds of flour and milk & spices, boiled in fresh lard, till they assume a beautiful fawn colour, are still my favorites. They can at any time maintain a rivalship even with sister Belle's soft ginger bread—on which, however, as it's *"past 12 O'c'k & a starlight morning,"* I mean presently to make an early breakfast.

Sat. 8ᵗʰ—3 P.M. This morning we had a second funeral procession from the Hall of our University. If I could record the names of all I have known to die, after having entered on the study of medicine since I began it, what a long and solemn catalogue would testify of God's goodness to *me*, in the length of *happy* days, with which I have been blessed. I was happy in the days of childhood which I am describing, and have lived long enough to find happiness in recurring to them — a delightful fountain of enjoyment, which time, when it mercifully smites the rock, opens to us. In the long period from youth to age, I had my trials and troubles, it is true; but I was in a stage of transition from one state of society to another; from the rural to the civic, from the rude to the refined, from obscurity to notoriety! The *caste* to which I belonged was to be changed; and in the arrangements of Providence, I was made, unconsciously, the instrument by which that change was to be effected. The conception of this change was less my own than my father's. He was a gentleman by nature, and a Christian from convictions produced by a simple & unassisted study of the word of God. His poverty he regretted; his ignorance he deplored. His natural instincts were to knowledge, refinement, and honorable influence in the affairs of the world. In consulting the traditions of the family he found no higher condition than his own as their lot in past times; but he had formed a conception of something *more* elevated, and resolved on its attainment; — not for himself and mother, nor for *all* his children — either would have been impossible — but for some member of the family. He would make a beginning; he would set his face toward the land of promise, although, like Moses, he himself should never enter it. Imperfectly as I have fulfilled the destiny which, under the arrangements of Providence, he assigned to me, I can not doubt that if he and mother should be permitted to look down upon the family group to whom you will read this epistle, they would gratefully exclaim — "The cherished desire of our hearts will at *last* be gratified!" But I have wandered far from the narrative in which I was engaged, and must return.

When I look back upon the useful arts which mother & I were accustomed to practice, I am almost surprised at their number and variety. Although I did not then regard them as anything but incidents of poverty and ignorance, I now view them as knowledge—as elements of mental growth. Among them was *colouring*. A "standing" dye stuff was the inner bark of the white walnut, from which we obtained that peculiar & permanent shade of dull yellow—the "Butternut," so common in these days. The "hulls" of the *black* walnut gave us a rusty black. Oak bark, with copperas as a mordant (when father had money to purchase it) afforded a better tint of the same kind, and supplied the ink with which I learned to write. Indigo, which cost eighteen pence an ounce, was used for blue; and madder, when we could obtain it at three shillings a pound, brought out a dirty red. In all these processes I was once almost an adept. As cotton was not then in use in this country (or in Europe) and flax can with difficulty be coloured, our material was generally wool or linsey or linsey woolsey; and this brings me once more to the flock.

It was common, as a preparation for shearing, to drive the sheep to some pond or stream, where there was sufficient water, that which was running answered best, and wash the wool while on their backs. Too weak to hold and wash a sheep, it was my function to assist in driving, and to keep the flock together at the water's edge; no very easy task, from their instinctive aversion to that fluid. Yet such a labour was a frolic, and broke in upon the lonely routine of daily life at home. In the shearing I could do something more, for then the animal is thrown upon the ground and tied. At 11 or 12 I could handle the shears very well, and felt proud of the accomplishment. The shearing and weighing done, then came the very different task of "picking." At that time, our little fields were badly cultivated, and whether the sheep were kept up or suffered to run at large in the woods, their wool became matted with cockle & other burs, which could only be disentangled with the fingers. In this wearisome labour, I have toiled through many a long rainy day, with my sisters and sometimes father or mother around the same fleece. There is no labour of boyhood that I look back upon with less satisfaction than this.

To the carding I lent a cheerfuller helping hand, and could roll out as many good rolls in a given time as any "*gaal*" of the neighbourhood. Mother generally did the spinning; but the "double & twisting" was a work in which I took real pleasure. The "buz" of the "big wheel" rising (as I walked backwards & turned the rim with increased velocity) from the lowest to the highest note of the octave, still seems like music in my ear. To this process succeeded the reeling into **skeans,** & at a future time, the winding of a part of these into balls, for stockings. In the last operation, I got my first lesson of patience under perplexity. When a tangled **skean** fell into my hands, fretfulness and impatience, its first fruits, were utterly at war with progress. Alas, how long it takes us to become submissive to such simple teachings.

In the long and checkered life through which I have passed since those days, how many tangled **skeans** have fallen into my hands, and how often have I forgotten the patience which my dear mother then inculcated upon me. Human life itself is but one long and large tangled **skean,** and in untwisting one thread we too often involve some others more fatally. Death, at last, unentangles all. To the eye of common observation the spacious firmament appears not less a tangled, than a shining frame, and yet, Newton, by *patience*, as he himself declared, reduced (for the human mind) the whole to order. When your husband was of the same age with myself, when I was taking my practical lessons of self control and constancy, he wrote to me from a distant school that he had adopted for his motto through life, "Patience and perseverance conquer all difficulties." I cannot repeat the foreign language in which he expressed it but *can* testify to the presage of the future and the pleasure at the present, which it inspired. It is delightful to see that time and experience have but brightened this *golden* maxim.

I must pass to a different topic, but one naturally suggested. I have in a former letter spoken of my labours with father in the flax patch, at the "break," and the "swingling board." With mother I hatcheled out the tow, and prepared in "knots" the beautiful fibre for the distaff, but never learned to spin on the "little wheel." Returned from the loom, the linen and "tow linen" was to be "whitened," and then my labours recommenced. If the "pulling," "spreading out to rot," & "breaking" were dirty and distasteful drudgeries, the labours of the bleachery were pleasant and picturesque. In the morning unrolling the linen on the green grass, & fastening down the corners with loops & sticks, carrying pure water from the spring, and sprinkling it out with the hand—for we were long without a "watering pot"—repeating the operation hour after hour, and carrying in the rolls at night, were labours which kept the hands clean and the heart cheerful. Is it not universally true that clean hands tend to give a cheerful heart? Then there was the high summer sun imprinting its pure light into the fabric, which every evening assumed a whiter and brighter hue. Last, and not least, was the joyous expectation of a couple of new shirts.

In many of the labours I have described, and many more with which I can not find it in my heart to trouble you, my sweet and gentle sister Lizzy was my companion and assistant. I never knew a kinder hearted child, one more ready and bent on dividing every good thing, and as far as I can now judge, I never loved a woman more tenderly. My very first memory was of her, and her death, while my patient, just 30 years afterwards was a sad affliction.

"In my haste," I said I would trouble you no more, but am already about to violate my promise. Our ages were too near for me to be her nurse, but my early remembrances disclose to me, that as soon as she was old enough to be amused, I was employed in that duty, and that as she advanced, I took an out door charge of her. Subsequently we were employed in common, rocking the cradle, carrying about, "tending" and taking care of the four younger children, while mother was at work. In this way I became quite a nurse, and may to it ascribe some of my traits of character in after life, which have been sources of both pleasure and profit. I like the society of little children, and their amusements around me excite and interest me, even when I do *not observe* them. I love to hear their voices — their young laughter cheers me — and their crying, if not from real grief, gives me but little disturbance of thought or feeling. Above all, I am delighted to see them aim at becoming members of an older circle, attentive to what is said, and anxious to ask a question or to put in a word. After saying this, you will not be surprised when I tell you that I have read many an hour with your husband and sisters, in my arms, often walking with them, and sometimes singing to keep them quiet. *Their* mother [meanwhile], in our poverty . . ., was at work in the kitchen or the chamber, alone, or with some miserable servant, such as Cincinnati had. Then the soft fibres of my younger heart were interwoven . . . with those of that lovely and beloved woman — so long my devoted companion in the cares and troubles and enjoyments of life. Had I not, in boyhood, been employed in the care of children, I should, in all probability, have lost afterwards many a day which I was able, as it was, to devote to study.

In a log cabin, one story high, 16 by 20 feet and without a partition, the distance from the nursery to the kitchen is not very great; and hence I am brought by a natural transition from nursing to *cooking!* Apropos — when dining yesterday with Dr Todd, as mentioned at the beginning of this long letter, he told Mrs Breckinridge, that in 1806, when he and Dr Richardson, Dr **Farrer,** and myself descended the Ohio together from Pittsburg in a flat boat, *I was the cook* — a fact which I had forgotten. This proved two others: —

first, that I knew something of the art; & second, that they did not. Neither assertion demands much proof, for my father was poor & *theirs* were either wealthy or in easy circumstances, and owned slaves. That I was strongly *inclined* to take the culinary department into my own hands, I can readily believe. Throughout my whole life, I have had an inveterate repugnance to a disordered kitchen and dirty cooks. At that time, when I was but 20 years old, I had mingled little with the world, and probably felt proud of my superior culinary accomplishments. It seems most likely that no feeling of an opposite kind existed in my bosom, or I should have remembered it.

I do remember one mortification of that voyage. When we were approaching Maysville, we began to dress up and prepare for landing. Each put on his best clothes, and I recollect that your friend D[r] **Farrer** especially exerted himself, because, as I suppose, he had relatives in the neighbourhood of the town. I also put on *my best* coat — that is — my *coat,* worn on a horseback journey of 18 days in the fall — for four months in Phil[a], and over the mountains to Pittsburg in the spring, to say nothing of cooking in it through a flatboat voyage of 10 days. The contrast it made with theirs gave me a feeling of mortification, which I have occasionally *recollected* ever since.

Could I have looked into the distant future, that feeling would have been annihilated; for I should have discovered that if the morning sun shines more brightly on some, the evening beams of that impartial luminary fall in greater mellowness on others. I should have seen, that 40 years afterwards, one would be in his grave [Dr. Wm. H. Richardson], after having almost had his heart broken by an only child, to whom he could not even venture to bequeath the remnants of an estate which had been squandered on or by that profligate son. I should have seen another, [Dr. Bernard G. Farrar, Sr.], retired from his profession with a shattered constitution, and worse spirits, without habits of intellectual cultivation, deprived of his best and oldest children, and falling out of sympathy with the society around; whence his old friends were dropping away one by one, without being replaced by new ones; as the jewels fall from the crown of a decayed monarch, who is too poor to replace them. I should have seen the third, as I saw him yesterday, with a wrinkled and sallow face, false hair, and green **gogly** spectacles, unsettled in place & purpose, his sons in Mexico & California, his wife dead, and not a daughter by *birth, marriage* or *adoption,* to care for and caress him. Yet, it is pleasant to add, I should have seen them all either dying or living in the Christian faith. But I must return to the family fireside — the infant school of all civilization.

I know of no scene in civilized life more primitive than such a cabin hearth as that of my mother. In the morning, a buckeye backlog & hickory forestick resting on stone andirons, with a **Jonny** cake on a clean ash board, set before it to bake, a frying pan with its long handle resting on a split bottomed turner's chair, sending out its peculiar music, and the tea kettle swung from a wooden "lug pole" with myself setting the table, or turning the meat, or watching the **Jonny** cake, while she sat nursing the baby in the corner, and telling the little ones to "hold still" and let their sister Lizy dress them! Then came blowing the conch-shell for father in the field, the howling of old Lion, and the momentary application of the shell to my ear, to hear the roaring of the sea, which, like all things in that fathomless profound, was a great mystery. Then came the gathering round the table—the blessing—the dull clatter of pewter spoons in pewter basins, the talk about crops and stock, the inquiry whether Dannel could be spared from the house, and the general arrangements for the day.

Breakfast over, my function was to provide the "sauce" for dinner. In winter, to open the potato or turnip "hole," and wash what I took out—in spring, to go into the fields and collect the "greens;" in summer and autumn, to explore the "truck patch," or our little garden; and from among the weeds dig or pull whatever might be in season. If I afterwards went to the field, my culinary labours ceased till night. If not, they continued through the day, and consisted of a participation in all that was going on—now tending the "child"—now hunting eggs to boil—now making up the fire —now sweeping up the hearth, and putting things to rights —now cleaning the old iron candle stick—now looking at the sill of the front door, to see by the shadow of one of its cheeks, whether it was time I should put the potatoes in— now twisting a fork in the meat to know if it were nearly done & now "fetching" a pail of fresh water, that father might wash his hands and take a drink.

At night, all *without* being attended to, and the family collected, the iron mush pot must be swung and supplied with water. Mother, or Lizzy (when old enough) generally stirred in the meal, but Dannel often stirred the mush. This was, of course, a standing dish for the younger children, but father and mother drank their bohea, (and abominable stuff it was; after a while, however, they reached the greater luxury of hyson-skin.) As often as possible, mother would engage in making pumpkin pies, in which, *con amore,* I generally bore a part. One of these more commonly graced the supper than the dinner table. At the proper season, "wonders" made our supper, and although I never made the dough, I was quite *au fait* in lifting them, at the proper time, out of the boiling fat, and equally adroit in **managing** them *at the table*.

But my labours as assistant nurse and cook were to have an end, if my narrative of them should not. When I was about 12 years old, and sister Lizy was 10, and father and mother began to find assistance from us at the same time. Still, up to my departure from home to study medicine at 15, my old functions were performed, more or less, on rainy days & Sundays, on wash days, and every night and morning. My pride was in the labours of the field, but taste and duty held me, as occasion required, to the duties of the house.

The time *has* been (*perhaps* should be still), when I looked back upon the years thus spent as *lost*. Lost as it respects my destiny in life — lost as to distinction in my profession — lost as to influence in the generation to which I belong. But might I not have been rocked in the cradle of affluence, been surounded by servants and tutors, exempt from every kind of labour, and indulged in every lawful gratification, and yet have at last fallen short of the limited and humble respectability which I now enjoy? In the half century which has elapsed since I began to emerge from those duties, I have certainly seen many who, enjoying all that I have named, still came to naught—were blighted, and if they did not fall from the parent bough, could not sustain themselves after the natural separation, but perished when they were expected to rise in strength and beauty. Who can tell that such might not have been my fate? The truth is, that I was the whole time in a school (I will not *any longer* say, of adversity, but) of probation and discipline, and was only deprived of the opportunities afforded by the school of letters. Great and precious as these are to him who is afterwards to cultivate literature and science, they are not the whole. They impart a certain kind of knowledge and strengthen the memory, but they leave many important principles of our nature undeveloped, and, therefore, can not guarantee future usefulness or fame.

I was preserved from many temptations, and practically taught self denial because indulgence, beyond certain narrow limits, was so much out of the question as not to be thought of. I was taught to practice economy, and to think of money as a thing not to be expended on luxuries, but to be used for useful ends. I was taught the value of learning, by being denied the opportunities for acquiring more than a pittance. I was taught the value of time, by having more to do day after day than could well be accomplished. I was molded to do many things, if not *absolutely* at the same time, in such quick succession as almost to render them identical—a habit which I have found of great advantage to me through life. But better than all these, I grew up with love and obedience to my mother, and received from her an early moral training, to which, in conjunction with that of my father, I owe, perhaps, more of my humble success in life, and of my humble preparation for the life to come, than to any other influence.

[My mother] was still more illiterate than my father but was pious, and could read the Bible, Rippon's hymns, and the Pilgrim's progress. Her natural understanding was tolerable only, but she comprehended the principles of domestic and Christian duty, and sought to inculcate them. This she never did by protracted lectures, but mixed them up with all our daily labours. Thus my monitor was always by my side, and ready with reproof, or admonition, or rewarding smile, as occasion required or opportunity arose. Unlike many (so called *wiser*) teachers, she instructed me as to what was *sin*. Her theory of morals was abundantly simple — *God has said it!* The Bible forbids this, and commands that, and God will punish you if you act contrary to his word! What philosopher could have risen so high? How simple & yet how sublime!

How often did I, and my sisters and brothers hear that impressive word *wicked* fall from her lips in the midst of her toilsome and never ceasing household duties! How seldom does it fall on the ears of many children, born under what are called happier auspices! It was wicked to treat anything which had life with cruelty—it was wicked to neglect the cattle or forget the little lambs in winter—it was wicked to waste or throw away bread or meat—it was wicked to strike or quarrel with each other, & this reminds me that Dr Watts' hymns for children was one of her small shelf of books. She had taught me to commit them to memory while yet a small boy. It was wicked to be lazy — to be disobedient — to work on the sabbath — to tell a false-hood, to curse and swear — to get drunk, or to fight. To this last she had a constitutional repugnance, not less than a moral. To [our similarity] of temperament, not less than to her precepts, I may ascribe that peaceful timidity of character, which often painfully embarrassed me in boy-hood, but at the same time preserved me from many scenes of violence & profanity. As I got older my temperament began to change toward that of my father & continues to advance in that direction — just as happens with your husband.

As you never saw my mother, even in her advanced age, permit me to add something to what you will collect of her person & character from what I have said. The crayon profile which hangs in Dove's room, taken when she was 60 years old, is correct in its anatomy, but the expression of countenance is too sad. In youth she must have been pretty if not beautiful. Her complexion, until she was 40 years of age, was the most delicate I ever saw. Till then, her health was, in general, good, and her industry and endurance very great. In this last, I claim some participation. Her temper was equable, her courage small but her fortitude great. Her spirits [were] less liable to depression than those of father; for if he lost a horse, he would, perhaps, take to his bed for a day. His health, however, was generally feeble, and his feelings most acute — so that he rose to higher gaiety and sunk to lower gloom, than mother. She relied on what she supposed [were] his greater knowledge & sounder judgment, and yet, although both were perhaps realities, his natural talents were not great, his acquirements were moderate, and his business enterprise small. His personal courage and his spirit were of a decided character when he was aroused; but he lacked moral courage, and was not only prone to hypochondraism, but afraid to engage in undertakings which were practicable. Above all, he was laudably afraid of going into debt, and gave me many admonitions, which I too little remembered in my after life.

In all the counselings of mother which I have enumerated, except what relates to *fighting*, father concurred, and exhorted and instructed me in every moral duty when we were in the field, as she was wont to do when I was with her in the house. They loved each other tenderly, lived in the greatest harmony, and, in reference to the government of the family made it an inviolable rule never to appear to differ.

Notwithstanding all this, there were three things in which I think father erred: *First*. He used to recount for our amusement his capers, frolics, and tricks when he was a young man, and, as it seems, rather wild. *Second*. He had a good-natured way of playing of jokes and jeers on mother when she, on any occasion, displayed ignorance or fear; which, it seems to me, *might* have had the effect of diminishing our respect for her character. *Third*. Although continuing a pious man till death, and yielding up his spirit in peace & hope, he gradually discontinued family worship, after practicing it for many years. This took place after I left home, at what time I do not know, nor did I ever learn the reason. My conjecture, however, is, that being illiterate and incapable of expressing himself in a satisfactory manner, as his children got older, he was embarrassed, as many fathers are, who never use a form of prayer.

In 1828, when I was ill and greatly depressed, I asked him (while we were alone) to pray with and for me, which, with evident emotion, he declined, saying that a form of words was nothing. It was this, in part, which suggested the conclusion which I have expressed. If that conclusion be correct, I would say that written forms of family prayer ought to be kept and occasionally used in every family. The father might often be in a frame of mind to render them acceptable; and in his absence or sickness or after his death, the mother might keep up family worship, which is generally then suspended—though more than ever required.

And now, my dear daughter, it is one o'clock A.M., and I have written to you through 10 successive hours. But, if you will fancy to yourself your dear little Austin, 60 years from this, engaged in giving to his children and grandchildren some account of you and his father, & of your influences in the formation of his character, you will at once excuse me for all that I have done.

That heaven will bless and prosper you, and those of your house, and all the dear brothers and sisters (including the Adopted) to whom you will read this wayward and wandering epistle, is the earnest prayer of your affectionate

Father

NATURE AS PRESCRIPTION

THE SETTING

The letter following is in reality a prescription written especially for his "adopted" daughter. Miss Belle Graham "apparently had a chronic case of nerves." Thus the letter may be read as an exhortation to forget her imaginary ills through the enjoyment to be found in nature.

Letter Six

NATURE AS PRESCRIPTION

To Miss Belle Graham[1]

Louisville, [Kentucky]
Jany 10th 1848, Monday P.M.

My Adopted Daughter:

According to the New Testament, this life is a state of Probation — a view which lies at the bottom of Bishop Butler's Analogy. It is not, however, one long monotonous trial, but a complex succession of cases, varying exceedingly in kind and degree. When a man is, by a casualty, thrown upon his back for 2 or 3 years, and compelled to earn his daily bread with his brow turned toward the heavens instead of the earth. . ., and has to hold up his hands till they tire like those of the Jewish lawgiver. . ., he is in probation. His courage, resignation, fertility of resource, and equanimity are on trial. The probation at the same time extends to his wife, whose love, patience, consideration, activity, temper, and ready sympathy are tested. When a professional man removes to a new position, & is thereby thrown out of business for awhile, his fortitude,

---

[1] Miss Belle Graham, a patient of Dr. Drake's and an intimate friend of his daughters. She spent much time in their homes and was called his adopted daughter. Wide search has failed to unearth either her portrait or the dates of her birth and death.

address, amenity, good nature, ingenuity, and hope are subjected to trial; and again, the wife has various traits of her character brought to the test. When a woman, in the necessary absence of her husband, has the care and government of the household devolved upon her, in the depth of a bleak and stormy winter, her skill in domestic economy & the discipline of children & servants, her decision, bravery, discretion, & fidelity, are on trial. When her husband, during his absence, is surrounded by the scenes and schemes of trade and speculation, and kept in suspense, and from home much longer than he desires, his sagacity, self control, integrity, prudence, & faithfulness are tried. When a young lady is adopted into a family, her tastes, accommodativeness, propriety of deportment, purity, active sympathy, and good sense are the subjects of her probation; and according to the result the adoption dies out, or at some future time is declared permanent.

While we resided in Mayslick, up to my 9th year, I saw, as I have said to Harriet, a great many people and a great many things and events; for our cabin was in the center of the station and by the side of the great road. To the village scenes I shall recur before I close my letter. At present you must regard us as in the depths of the woods, though only a mile from our late residence. When we first went thither, there was but a single family within a mile of the spot, though at that distance there were new settlers on every side. To the south, imperfectly in sight of our "new home" there was a narrow & winding road, along which the neighbours from the west traveled to the village. Father opened another to the Pond a mile west of us, near which there were settlers, and thus brought a feeble current of folk through our own lane near to our house. Now, among my liveliest recollections was the pleasure which mother & the children enjoyed when any one came in sight. For the first years, she felt the solitude in which we were entombed, more severely than any other member of the family. She could not go much from home, like father whom business would frequently call away, nor like myself, who was the errant boy, and therefore, sent frequently into the "Lick" & to our neighbours, from the first day of our removal. The children, moreover, had their plays and rambles in the little fields & adjoining woods, which were close at hand; and children are not less amused than benefited by straying among natural objects. To revel in them is one of their instincts.

If I were to write a *recipe* for making great and good men and women, I would direct the family to be placed in the woods — reared on simple food — dressed in plain clothes — made to participate in rural and domestic employments — allowed to range through the groves & thickets, but *required a part of every day to give themselves up to the instruction of competent and accomplished teachers,* till they were 14 or 16 years of age. In my case the last element was wanting; and, therefore, you must not judge of my system by myself. Had that desideratum been supplied, there is no knowing but that I might, ere this, have edited an edition of the Iliad with notes, or written commentaries on Aristotle! Perhaps, I might even, at this moment have been at Washington, intriguing for the presidency, instead of lecturing as I did today on Dyspepsia, and writing about bird's nests, pawpaws, and old ladies riding along "bridle paths" on men's saddles, as I am doing tonight.

The very loneliness of our situation led me to seek for new society & amusement in the woods, as often as opportunity offered. But they were, in themselves, attractive. To my young mind there was in them a kind of mystery. They excited my imagination. They awakened curiosity. They were exhaustless in variety. There was always something ahead. Some new or queer object *might be* expected, and thus anticipation was sustained. To go from the family fireside—from the midst of large and little babies, and cats and kittens—into the woods for society, may seem to you rather paradoxical, but it was not so in fact. Familiar objects lost their wonted effect, and we may become solitary in their midst.

But, to find men in trees, and women in bushes, and children in the flowers, and to be refreshed by them, one must be a little imaginative, and so I was, as I *now* know, though I did not know it then. To frequent the woods from motives of *mere utility* is *mere occupation,* and all the feeling raised by it is that which is connected with business. With this also I was well acquainted, for I was often sent to search out a tree or sapling for some special purpose, as, to make a helve or a basket (of which I have plaited many, & could now earn my living by it); or bottom a chair (which I have often done); or to make a broom (of which I have already bragged). But an excursion in spring to gather flowers was a very different affair. I am unable to analyse the emotions which these excursions raised in me; but the pleasure on finding a new flower was most decided, and hence, a strange and retired locality was a spot of the deepest interest. On approaching it my imagination became excited, and filled it with all possible novelties. Ten years afterwards, when I got a book or two on Botany and took them into the woods of Mount Adams[2] a name, by the way, which *I* proposed for the hill on which the observatory stands), these same early friends came before me in a new aspect, and sweetened even the perplexities which attended their scientific examination with the incompetent works by which I attempted it. Still the Claytonias, Pulmonaries, Phloxes, Trilliums, & Fringillarias, whose annual reappearance I had greeted in each succeeding spring of my boyhood, were my favorite subjects of botanical investigation. Twenty years after I had held this *second* communion with them, when I unexpectedly came upon some of them in the Botanic Garden attached to Harvard University, they seemed like old & early friends in a strange land.

Summer had its charms not less than spring. Its flowers, its luxuriant herbage, its blackberries & wild cherries, its endless variety of green leaves, its deep and cool shade, with bright gleams of sunshine, its sluggish & half dried up brooks, of which, like other boys, I would lie down and drink (first looking out for snakes), and then turn over the flat stones, to see if there were any crawfish beneath. Both seasons had their squirrels and ground squirrels; the former skipping from tree to tree in chase of each other, or seated

---

[2] Mount Adams, the hill upon which the Cincinnati Observatory was erected. The corner stone was laid on November 9, 1843, by John Quincy Adams.

basking with their tails turned over their backs; the latter dodging over the trunk of some fallen tree, and at length hiding beneath. The same seasons had their birds, whose notes made a symphony with the winds, while they played upon the green leaves & awakened melody as when the rays of the sun fell upon the harp of Memnon, but more real, and better for the young heart. Then there were nests with speckled eggs, suspended from the limbs of trees, or formed, as those of the woodpecker, in a decayed trunk, or fixed in the depths of some inaccessible briery. To take home the eggs, blow them out, and string them *into* beads for Lizy, was a supplementary work.

My summer rambles presented still other objects well fitted to raise emotion and impart knowledge. A fallen tree, nearly decayed, with flowers smiling out of its ruins; another, less decomposed, with beautiful boles, lichens & other *imperfect* parasitic plants adhering to it, while the wood within was the food of grubs and worms; another still, dissolved into mold & covered with rank weeds & grass. What beautiful lessons on the course and economy of nature! And yet how seldom studied by the children of our cities!

Another tree stricken by the lightning—its bark peeled off and scattered around—or its trunk split from top to bottom, and its leaves wilted—or quite withered and rustling in the breeze, for when thus destroyed, the leaves do not fall off. Many trees prostrated, blown up by the roots, or broken off at various heights, lying twisted and tangled on the ground, the victims of a tornado which had swept through the forest, like an epidemic through society.

What an appeal to the emotions of sublimity and terror in the young mind! Well do I remember the tempests by which this desolation was effected. Often have I run from the woods to escape the danger. Still oftener have I witnessed from our log cabin the thunder storms of July and August. They who have only heard & seen them in the midst of a dense city population while sitting in houses protected by lightning rods, know nothing of the emotions they raise while sweeping over a solitary cabin, with a corn field on one side and a wilderness on the other. A storm of this kind fell upon us oftener in August than any other month. After a breathless and sultry noon, piles of black & white clouds would appear overhead, as if let down from the heavens. It puzzled me to tell where they came from. In the west, from the zenith to the horizon, they became heavier and blacker, furnishing a dark background to the landscape of green trees which stood quiet and unconscious, or, in a momentary breeze, shuddered in every leaf, as if awake to the impending danger. A few rolls of distant thunder, or a dim streak of lightning (a signal fire of the sky) hurried us from the field. The cattle and horses, as if conscious of the danger which awaited their remaining among the dead trees left in our inclosure, would slowly collect on the spots where they were fed at night. On reaching the house, mother and the children would be occupied in setting out every vessel that could be spared, to "catch" rain water, and in carrying in the clothes or whatever else would be injured by the rain. All things were now arranged, and the tempest with its louder artillery and more vivid flashes was at hand. God was present in the storm.

Both Father and mother became solemn and the Bible was sometimes laid open and read. The children were admonished & instructed. We might be destroyed; but another and purer emotion blended with our fears — a feeling of reverence converting terror into awe. We were in the midst of a great and sudden visitation of Divine power. We heard a voice, as it were, from Heaven. Down, even to this distant and **waining** time of life, a thunderstorm brings back the solemn thoughts and emotions of those hours of elemental sublimity without and *moral* sublimity within, the lone & humble family dwelling. The world (if that great personage knew what I am writing) might call this superstition. I shall never debate the matter with him, but cleave to the feeling and give thanks, that it was so implanted in my heart by pious parents, that his pestiferous breathings can never blight it.

But the tempest was over and all around us. The dry & low cabin roof was the sounding board of the big drops, often intermingled with hail stones, and to this moment the music of the shower exerts on me a more delightful influence than any other. Lightnings, which seemed like those of **Sinia,** burst from the black cloud, and the angel of the storm sounded his trumpet in explosions so loud & sudden as to raise vibrations in every log of the cabin and tremors in every heart within. The corn, with its half grown ears, bent to the earth before the wind, much of it unable to rise again, and much of it destroyed by the fall of dead trees left in the field. A few solitary green trees left near the spring would bow and wave gracefully in the wind, & perhaps lose a limb, under the shade of which the children had been playing but an hour before. If the movements of a solitary tree in the midst of the tempest are beautiful, the struggles of the forest are sublime. Encumbered with a mighty weight of leaves, it groaned and struggled under the whirlwind, like a mother who seeks to sustain herself and little one, against the storms of adversity. The young trees would bend low, but rise with the flexibility of youth—older ones were driven against each other with a terrible crash, and have their branches interlocked or torn off. The aged & unbending were broken and fell, carrying with them to the earth and burying up their younger companions & their own offspring.

The dark cloud at length passed on to the east and was illuminated with broad flashes of lightning. The thunder rumbled in the distant horizon & the declining sun began to beam in the west. The rainbow, diadem of the viewless messenger of mercy and repose, would rest its extremities on the still quivering woods; while the smiling freshness of the green leaves declared their sympathy with the safe and joyous inmates of the cabin.

Now was the time to leave it for the fields, to see what injury had been done & what must be, at once repaired, to preserve the crops from the depredations of the stock. I well recollect how wonder and curiosity now took the place of terror. Every thing wore a new aspect, and told of the hurricane. The corn was often so far inclined to the earth that on the following day it must be righted up with the hoe; dry trees were blown up by the roots, destroying much on which we had toiled. In one instance a magnificent white oak, which had been left ungirdled, and in the shade of which I had often sat down to rest, or leaned on the handle of my hoe, was stricken by lightning, and its limbs and splinters lay scattered around. Partition fences were occasionally blown down, and the outside fences crushed by the fall of great trees from the adjoining woods. Here were new and added labours, but the feelings connected with them were tinctured with those which the storm had inspired, and gave to the work, as I well remember, a kind of romantic interest.

The "Fall," as we always called it, not less than spring and summer, brought its sylvan scenes and pleasures; but do not for a moment suppose that the foreign adjective I have just employed was a word of *those* days, or that "autumn" & "forest" made a part of our vocabulary. All was *rudely* vernacular, and I knew not then the meaning of that word. We spoke a dialect of old English, in queer pronunciation and abominable grammar. After I left home, and began to read books, abounding, as those of my profession did, at that day more than the present, in long and lumbering words derived from Greek and Latin roots, it was not unnatural, I think, that I should become enamoured of them, and seek to escape upon them from the vulgarisms of my mother tongue. In the progress of time better views came into my mind, and a reaction took place; but it was too late, and up to this very epistle (the word should have been *letter*) I find them *intrusively precluding* more *appropriate* Anglo-Saxon **synonims.**

The autumn, as I was about to say, often called me to the woods, and united the useful with the romantic. It was not to cut broom sticks, or select a tree for rails or clap-boards, but to gather those wild fruits which were so precious to us in the absence of the cultivated. Some of them were for immediate use, or little thought of except by the children; others had a more permanent value, and were stored for winter. Among the former I may mention hack-berries, pawpaws, plums, haws, & honey locust pods. Among the latter, grapes, nuts, crab apples, and occasionally the hard seeds of the coffee tree (guylandina Bonduc),[3] of which, by way of change from Bohea tea, we made a substitute for coffee. Hackberries and locust pods, or rather the deposit of sweet pulp which the latter contain, were chiefly eaten by the children, who relished them as delicious. The plums were commonly sour, but not so acerb as to kill *all* the worms. The pawpaw was a general favorite, though mother never ate it; & many persons, then & since, I have observed, have the same infirmity of taste. To me they were always luscious; and to go into the woods after the first frosts, with a basket on my arm and old Lion trotting before me, was, beyond all dispute, a trip of pleasure. In this fruit I became, and remain, a greater *connoisseur* (oh, these vile foreign words) than any other. I can tell their characters by their outside, much better than that of men and women. There are two varieties, the pale yellow & the white. The latter are intolerable to all tastes, until they have been frostbitten half a dozen times. I observed that but two animals ate the pawpaw — ants and opossums.

[3] The Kentucky coffeetree (the Kentucky mahogany), to which he refers, is today designated the *Gymnocladus dioica* (L.) Koch, (*G. canadensis* Lam.)

All attempts to use them in cookery were unavailing.

To gather haws was another attractive labour. There were several varieties. A haw tree, always small, when its bright red fruit was fully ripe, made quite a show, and the haw gave us a very tolerable substitute for the apple, to which it has a close botanical affinity. But the greatest charm of haw hunting was found in the favorite locality of that tree, always on the margin of some rocky brook, along which it was delightful to saunter, and see the minnows frisk about in its pools, or a harmless water snake hide under the edge of some projecting stone.

Grapes for present eating were obtained by climbing small trees, an art in which I acquired considerable skill; and in the practice of which I tore the knees of many a pair of pantaloons, when they were not made of buckskin. At a later period of autumn came the greater vintage when they were obtained for tarts and preserves by chopping down the trees, in the fall of which, if they were overripe, they would, by the jar, be shaken off the stems. I was often subjected to this disappointment.

Crab apples were gathered after they had been exposed to the mellowing influences of a few white frosts. This tree, the color, form & odor of whose flowers are equally beautiful and delicious, was always found solitary (while the pawpaw formed groves or patches.) It was our great resource for preserves throughout the year—and certainly no cultivated fruit is better. In clearing land, this *lady like* tree was always spared. In giving it this dignified and endearing application [appellation], I refer, of course, to its moderate size and graceful form, to the beautiful tints and sweet aroma of its flowers, and *not to the acidity of its fruit.*

But my great forest labour in autumn was nut gathering—*hic labor, hoc opus est,* which, liberally translated, signifies that I had to take old Bob and a bag, or harnessing him with a straw collar and rope traces, or tugs of raw hide, hitch him to a log sled, with a washing tub tied upon it. Black walnuts were most abundant, and they made our staple; next came hickory nuts, and lastly, butternuts. These were stored up for the long and lonely winter nights, and it was generally my province, after supper, with the axe or a flat iron or a stone, to crack them for the whole family. Of course, I became skillful in what is rather a difficult art. Behold, then, the whole family arranged on chairs and stools around the great undressed hearthstone, each with a pewter plate in his lap and an iron fork, a "Barlow" penknife or the sharp blade of an old pair of scissors in his right hand; while long strips of hickory bark, crackling on the fire, kept up a light which illumined the happy faces of the family group.

The "Fall" was a hunting Season; but before I was old & large enough to traverse the woods with the instrument of death, deer and **turkies** had become scarce. I sometimes, however accompanied father on such excursions. My own performances were chiefly in squirrel hunting, and my first essays, as I have already said, were in and about the corn field. I began with the shot gun, but advanced to the rifle, in the use of which I became so good a marksman, as to be no contemptible match for some older than myself in shooting at a mark, one of the most fascinating sports of those days of physical pastime. I have often hunted squirrels for profit. I diminished their numbers and preserved our corn, on which they were disposed to prey in autumn. Their flesh supplied us with food; and I could sometimes barter their dried skins at Uncle Abraham Drake's store for "goods."

But Squirrel hunting, every now and then, took on the character of an organized and highly exciting frolic. The object of the old and sober minded men was the extirpation of that mischievous little animal; that of the younger, with boys and urchins, was sport and the excitement of competition. Many days were allowed for preparation, that all who chose to enter the lists might be adequately equipped. By common consent the gathering was made at some central house of the neighbourhood, & I well recollect that it was once at father's. The commencement was the morning, and the coming in from the woods was at an appointed time in the evening. The first step in the campaign was to divide the forces under two able leaders; between whom, of course, there arose an instant rivalship as to the number of scalps they might bring in; but the relative *general* aggregate was to decide who had the victory. The light troops were the boys and dogs, who attached themselves to the different hunters, according to consanguinity, affection, or confidence; and I observed at that early period (what I believe is, in modification, true of human nature generally), that the boys were most desirous of serving the best hunters. The dogs seemed to have some portion of the same instinct. It was the office of both to go through the woods and hunt up the game, keeping the cunning little animal in the eye, and be able to point him out to the hunter when he reached the spot. If the animal fell wounded, the dogs would catch & kill him; when one of the boys would scalp him, and string the scalp on a thread. Meantime, others had started forward, and as soon as the hunter had wiped and loaded his rifle,[4] he followed on. The scene throughout was one of absorbing interest, and the excitement continued to the very close; for, on the return of the various parties, the comparison of the trophies of rival hunters of the two commanders, the final summing up, and the proclamation of the victory raised an excitement which even made the hearts of the old men palpitate with greater force.

I come to a very different kind of hunting—solitary, sauntering, silent, and bloodless, yet demanding perservance, observation, and an accurate eye. I refer to *bee hunting*, to which my taste and temperament gave me a stronger inclination than to the murderous rifle. In hunting bees we went among the flowers, where they fill themselves with honey or load their bristly thighs with pollen to form their cells.[5] We often had a patch of Buckwheat, the flowers of which are highly attractive to them. At other times, father and I went into the woods, and sought them among their autumnal blossoms. A more efficient mode than either

[4] The Kentucky rifles of this period were flint-locks which required considerable time to wipe and reload. The calibre varied from .32 inch to approximately .60 inch and the barrels were unusually long, sometimes over 36 inches.

[5] Dr. Drake seems to assume that pollen is used to form the cells. This is, of course, erroneous. Bees collect pollen which, stored in cells, is used to feed their brood.

was to seek some open spot in the forest, and, striking a fire with "flint and steel" for lucifer matches were then unknown,[6] heat a small flat stone, and throw on it some honey comb. The treacherous incense rising among the trees, was to attract to the spot the unsuspecting little insect, if any should be near. Meanwhile we took our seats among the grass and flowers to muse or talk, while we kept a vigilant lookout for arrivals. . . When the bee has sucked its fill, it rises, makes two or three limited circuits, and then moves off in a straight—a "bee" line to the swarm [colony] of which it is a member. When we saw several pursue the same course we took it ourselves, and the *hunting* in the second stage was then begun.

The small & sound trees might be passed without inspection. The larger and older, hollow at the heart would alone be likely to afford a hive for the swarm. Around the opening into this the bees would be seen diligently flying in and out. Sometimes the tree could not be found, and then the rule was to send up new odour of the honey-comb, from a spot to the right or left of the line we had been exploring, and observe the course the insects took from it. Where the two lines would intersect, his habitation might be found. The pleasure of the discovery was very great, and the initials of the finder were inscribed on the bark of the tree.

To get the honey was often a kind of frolic, made up of a few friends or neighbours. When, as sometimes hap-

---

[6] The first friction match has devised in 1827 by an Englishman, John Walker. It was not readily inflammable. A young Frenchman, Charles Sauria, an apothecary's assistant, devised a satisfactory match with a phosphorous base in 1831.

pened, the swarm was in the limb of a large tree, and it projected so horizontally as to permit a man to stand upon it, I have seen him ascend to a great height and chop or saw it off. More commonly the tree was felled, and I have known large and noble oaks, not needed for timber, cut down for this purpose. By the fall, the hollow part would be shivered into fragments, the honey-comb mashed and scattered on the ground, and while a quart or two was hastily gathered up, its enraged and courageous little owners would be as busily occupied in punishing the plunderers. Thus would terminate the Bee hunt;—of which the pleasure is in the finding, and not the taking: in the anticipation, much more than the possession.

Jany 12th—P.M. Wednesday. Of winter scenes in the woods, I have spoken in some preceding letter, and will not chill you with any more. But, as it is still autumn, you must gaze for a moment at the hues in which the woods are so gloriously attired. This, it is true, you have often done, but not with that magical kaleidoscope, the mind's eye, through which I desire you now to inspect them. And yet I shall not attempt to paint them, but merely place before you some (suggestive) hints on their peculiarities & influence.

While yet unmutilated by the rude and powerful arm of the pioneer, the woods are a great school of beauty. There is a stern beauty in leafless winter, when, after a cold rain, the limbs and twigs are transformed to inverted icicles, on which the light of the cold bright sun plays in dazzling splendour.

There is a soft and smiling beauty in spring, when the tender leaves of every [tree], and the rival blossoms of the Buckeye, Dogwood, Red Bud, Crab apple & locust, unite in speaking to our hearts that the dominion of winter is at an end.

There is a ripe, aromatic and welcome beauty in summer, when the sun, once more a fountain of heat as well as light, has given breadth of form and depth of green to the leaves, & erected the woods into one vast temple, whose columns are the trees—whose covering is a leafy firmament.

In autumn there is a solemn and meditative beauty, when the canopy of foliage (like that tenant of the Deep which, laid upon the sands of the shore, radiates all the colours of the rainbow and then expires) puts on every hue and begins to fall. In this affecting display of mingled tints (which has no equal in nature, save that sometimes made in the clouds, for a moment, by the setting sun), a living green, here and there, still smiles upon us. The brown and withered leaves, which are already strewn around us, tell too plainly the end to which all are hastening. They have but gone before the rest, and the hand of the same destiny is suspended over all. Their course is run, their work is done and they are preparing to die. They no longer play together in the breeze, nor strive with each other for the sun. The fruit & seed which they had protected from rays, and helped to nourish, are now ripe, and must soon follow them to the parent earth—there to be defended by them from the frosts of winter, and at some future time become their food—be converted into wood & fruit—experience a resurrection, and take a new body. But without dwelling on this symbol of our own transition to a spiritual life, we may see in the series of autumnal events the care with which God has provided for the preservation and perpetuation of the forest races, by an endless multiplication of germs, and their dependence on the parent tree for life: on its leaves for protection, and the influence of air, to them the "breath of life"; — thus illustrating, in the midst of surpassing beauty & solemn grandeur, the relations of child and parent, and showing all to be the workmanship of one wise & almighty Hand.

Such are some of the autumnal lessons taught in the great school house of the woods. For that school house I had a passion which in boyhood never cloyed, and in age is not extinct. The scenes of those blessed days of autumn, not only rise fresh and living in my memory, but to this hour a solitary ramble in a retired and quiet wood, when the brown and yellow leaves are falling one by one around me, as the passing breeze breaks the last thread of their existence, is a cherished indulgence — a grave yet refreshing feast of the soul.

But, my dear child, do not for one moment suppose that I then had, or now pretend to have had, the thoughts and emotions which I am here expressing; for I know they were not present with me. What I contend for is, that to be in the midst of such scenes in childhood & youth is beneficial. I insist that autumn has its lessons for the mind, and its influences on the young heart, and that to many they are most precious. Children are seldom conscious of many of the effects which external circumstances produce upon them. They know when they are pleased & when displeased, but give no heed to the germs of thought, emotion and taste, which the scenes and objects around them may be quickening into life. They are unaware of the tendency which this influence is giving them to good or that to evil, and yet both may be a reality, a permanent bias. They are molded and may feel the hand, but know nothing of the model, which is in the mind of the artist. They assume a specific form but are not then, perhaps *never,* able to refer it to the impressing forces; & still, but for them, it would not have come into existence. That the autumnal influences of which I have spoken, were molding forces of my own character, and that many of its better traits were thus called into activity, I can not doubt. Having thus developed to you another agency which acted on me in boyhood (the proper object of my letter) I request you to generalize & extend what is true of one, to the character of many.

But you will perhaps ask, are there not multitudes who spend their whole lives in new countries, and yet die uninstructed in mind — unelevated in feeling, by the scenery around them? The answer is that this seems to be the case; but we know not, in their destitution of so many palpable sources of knowledge and refinement, how much that is good in their character would have been absent if this also had been wanting. Because they do not *speak* of the beauties, solemnities, and sublimities of nature, we are not to conclude that those attributes have exerted no effect upon them. They are grown up *children.* They do not analyse their own character, nor that of the influences which surround them, & to which indeed they give little of conscious attention; but God provides that his works shall affect us even while we neglect to examine and admire them.

But where am I? Whither have I wandered? Did I not announce at the beginning of my letter a different train of narrative from that on which I have dwelt through so many pages? Yes. I started with the design of revealing to you the social influences beyond the family circle which surrounded me in boyhood. I even began to speak of my longings after them; and then plunged into the deeper solitudes of the wilderness! What a strange vagary! I meant to introduce to you my comrades of the neighbouring log cabins, but presented in their stead, my silent companions of the intervening woods! For people I gave you trees! For dirty hearths, ragged boys, trollopy girls, and crying babies, I gave you green bowers & chirping birds. Well, be it so. On some, less or more fortunate member of the family group, the whole may sometime fall.

Till when, as ever after, I remain

your faithful & affectionate

Foster Father

SCHOOL OF THE WOODS

THE SETTING

Dr. Drake owed much to his mother and father for his education, both formal and informal. His father made every effort to keep him in school despite the great need for his services in the home and in the field. Poor as they were, the expenditure for books was out of all proportion to their meager income. Dr. Drake's education, in early as well as later life, was dependent upon his own reading which obviously was omnivorous. That his reading was careful and critical is evidenced by the penciled annotations and corrections in two volumes formerly owned by him and now in my collection, *The Natural History of Society,* by W. Cooke Taylor (2 vols., New York: D. Appleton & Co., 1841).

Letter Seven

SCHOOL OF THE WOODS

To Mrs. Alexander Hamilton McGuffey[1]

Louisville, [Kentucky]
Jan[y] 13th, 1848, Thursday P.M.

My Dear Dove,

When two years ago, on the 45th anniversary of my departure from home to study medicine, I yielded to the old man's
instinct to the past, and gave you in 12 or 14 pages, some
account of that departure—the transition to a new kind of
life—the beginning of a different career—I did not *intend*
(for I did not even debate the matter with myself) to follow
that letter up with any more of the same sort. Nevertheless,
I have done it this winter, till passing round the family circle
I have come to you, with whom I started, and now propose
to write you a second time. In my former letter I told you
that I was put to the study of medicine without the acquirements which are now made by the scholars of our most
ordinary public schools. Of the opportunities under which I
picked up what I knew, and of the want of opportunities for

[1] Dove, pet name for Elizabeth Mansfield Drake McGuffey (1817-1864),
older daughter of Dr. Drake. This letter, copied verbatim from the 1870
edition, was reprinted with an introduction by Mr. J. Christian Bay under
the title *Pioneer Education and Life* (The Torch Press, Cedar Rapids, Ia.,
Christmas 1939).

acquiring more, I propose, in the first part of this letter, to say something; allowing myself the privilege of digression & retrogression, not less than of progression.

In the fall of 1817, when, at the age of 5 months, you were taken in my and your dear mother's arms to Lexington, [Ky.], I going thither as professor of Materia Medica in Transylvania University, the Academical Department was not, like the medical, in a forming state; for, although low in condition & character, it had existed, I believe, for at least 25 years,[2] that is, from the time I was a "little boy." There were, moreover, classical & mathematical teachers scattered over the interior of that state, of whom I recollect the names of Filson,[3] one of the proprietors of Cincinnati, Sharp, Clark, & Stubbs; but never knew any except the last. In that part of Kentucky which lies north of Licking river — the counties of Mason, Fleming, & Bracken, however, there was not, as far as I can recollect, a single teacher of that kind. Most certainly there was none about Mayslick, and till after I commenced the study of medicine I never saw one of those distinguished personages. But had they been as numerous and cunning as the foxes which ate up our chickens, it would not have done me any great good, seeing that Father had

[2] In 1780 the General Assembly of Virginia set aside certain escheated Tory lands in the county of Kentucky for an endowment of a *seminary of learning*. The resulting institution, Transylvania Seminary, was merged with a rival one, the Kentucky Academy, in 1798 to form Transylvania University. At the first meeting of the Board of Trustees, medical and law departments were authorized in addition to the academic. However, it was not until the fall of 1817 that the medical department began to function.

[3] John Filson (1747-1788), a Pennsylvanian by birth, a schoolmaster by occupation, the first historian of Kentucky, an explorer of the central west and one of the founders of Cincinnati or, as he named it, Losantiville.

Elizabeth Mansfield Drake McGuffey

such urgent need of my assistance on the farm, that I could only have gone to school now & then; & seeing still further that he felt, & indeed *was,* too poor to pay more than "15 shillings" a quarter; a compensation for which a man of education would not have given his services.

The general rule as to my going to school was, to attend in winter, & stay at home for work the other parts of the year; but this was not rigidly observed. In my letter to "sister Echo," I have mentioned the names of McQuitty, Wallace, & Curry, as my teachers till I was 9 years old. Father then removed from the village, and my schooling was suspended. At the time it was broken off, I had luckily learned to read, and had begun to write large "joining hand," & make capitals. Thus I was able to make some progress at home; and about half a mile from us there was a youth of 16 or 18 who was a pretty good "penman" and when he visited us, used to set me copies and mend my pen . . . I regret that my memory has allowed his name to pass away. Our teachers should never be forgotten, and, above all, those who gratuitously come forward in our destitution.

Father and his neighbours were not indifferent to the education of their children; but they were all new settlers, all poor and all illiterate, & hence had not the means or conception necessary to the establishment of a good school, even had it been possible to procure a competent teacher. In a year or two after our removal a small log schoolhouse was erected by the joint labour of several neighbours, about half a mile north from his house, and just beyond the "line" of his "place." It was entirely in the woods, but one of the wagon roads leading into the "Lick" passed by its very door. In the winter, light was admitted through oiled paper by long openings between the logs; for at that time glass was not thought of. It was one story high without any upper floor, and about 16 by 20 feet in dimensions, with a great wooden chimney, a broad puncheon floor, and a door of the same material, with its latch and string. I give you these details, because they are equally descriptive of the "common run" of school houses at that time. I never heard a reason assigned for placing them, generally by the road side; but the travel was not great, and such was the insulation of families, that I fancy by common consent & mere social instinct, the children were placed under circumstances to see all that could be seen. Perhaps, as they occasionally saw new aspects of things and persons, it was the best plan. In the year 1836, a little more than 40 years after this schoolhouse was built, I took you and your sister to the spot. We found a ploughed field and no fragment of my first "sylvan academy."

The first teacher, who wielded the hickory mace in this *academy,* was *Jacob Beaden.* You will think his name in true harmony with the house. He was a recent immigrant from the "eastern shore" of Maryland, and an ample exponent of the state of society in that benighted region. His function was to teach spelling, reading, writing and cyphering as far as the rule of three; beyond which he could not go. His attainments in that branch harmonized as to quality and compass with his erudition in the others. The fashion was for the whole school to learn & say their lessons aloud, and a noisier display of emulation has perhaps never since been made. This fashion, in those days, was common to all our schools, and although, at first view, it may seem absurd and at variance with all improvement, something may be said on the other side.

1st Children are naturally prone to speak or utter audibly when they are learning. I think it an instinct of their minds, and if so, it is not absurd. The final cause or end, if it be instinctive, may be to improve their speech, and to impress the matter upon them through the medium of a second sense—their own hearing.

2d In silent study, an active and diligent child does not stimulate the more listless; but in audible study it does. When a boy would raise his voice and become more intense and rapid, others would do the same, and they would extend the impulse further, until the high excitement would be spread throughout the whole school. Master Beaden, the while, looked on with the satisfaction of one who sees his work going on with becoming energy.

3d The scholars, when accustomed to this mode of study, do not interrupt each other. They merely hear a noise, as Charlie hears the noises in the street, in front of Miss Bennett's school room. They do not apprehend what is said by those around them. Now, there is an advantage of a permanent kind in becoming accustomed in early life to do "head work" in the midst of noise. In reference to myself, it was perhaps the greatest which Master Beaden conferred upon me. It enabled me afterwards to prosecute my studies when you and Echo were talking, laughing, screaming, and crying round my table. It enables me to sit down and write or read in the midst of a steam boat hurleyburley. When I lodged in the University, there was at night a profound silence; where I now sit, only eight feet from a public street, and quite on its level, I hear the voices and footsteps of all the passers by, the play & shouts of boys, the loud & hearty laughter of negroes, and the rattle of drays & hacks, throughout the day & till 12 at night, and yet as far as I can judge, my mind is more active here than within those silent classic walls.

4th Children, like adults, when they sit still, breathe slowly, and their blood is not adequately purified by the atmosphere; which makes them nervous & **fidgetty.** But this is obviated by their studying aloud, when they must of necessity breathe a great deal.

5th By this exercise the vocal organs are strengthened; and in my own case, I may perhaps, trace up my capacity for long, loud, and rapid utterance (a good substitute in most cases for sound knowledge & accurate thinking) to my ample practice in the log school house.

So, you see, I can raise a snug little argument in favour of one of the customs of my boyhood, still prevalent in the new settlements, but proscribed, I believe, in the older. Silent study is solitary, but audible may be made social. This was much the case in Master Beaden's school.

Two boys or more would "get" & say their spelling lessons together, and so of their reading lessons. The spelling book was Dilworth's,[4] an old English production, which I would like to get hold of once more. The reading book was the

---

[4] Thomas Dilworth (died 1780), an English acountant and author of school books which had a wide sale in the eighteenth century. The spelling book to which Drake refers included a short grammar and also select quotations, divine, moral, and historical, together with forms of prayer for children.

New Testament, in which we read verse about. When the time for "letting out" was at hand, the whole school were called up to spell, & then came the strife of glory—the turning down & going up head.

When the dismissal was pronounced came the scramble for wool hats of all ages, sun bonnets, without pasteboard, of all materials, and dinner baskets of home manufacture. As the rush through the door was effected, the dispersion was invariably in a run with hopping, jumping, and halloing. I have never read one of the **Waverly** novels, but remember once to have looked into "Old Mortality," I think it was, at the house of a patient, and read in the opening chapter a description of the letting out of a country school in Scotland, which might have been drawn from that of Master Beaden's—so much are children alike in all countries.

Our school house was about 300 yards from the spring which supplied us with water. It was brought in a bucket by two boys; and the candidates for this duty were as numerous and as vigilant as the candidates for professorships in our medical schools. The path lay through the woods, and the trip was one of talk, stopping to rest, and looking hither and thither.

All the scholars brought their dinner, & it was generally a social meal, with cronies & squads on the benches in winter—on old logs in the adjoining woods, at other seasons. The meal over, then came the play & romps, in many of which the boys and girls mingled together; but sometimes the rudeness of the former drove the latter for one "dinner spell" by themselves. Swinging by grape vines was, in general, a joint amusement, as was hunting nuts, haws, pawpaws, & other fruits, when in season. The boys climbed trees after bird's nests, grapes, and for the enterprise. It was sometimes a matter of ambition to see who could climb the highest. Now and then several would ascend the same tree, and be clinging to its trunk at the same time; or two would start on opposite sides of one tree and strive for the greater elevation. Occasionally, a luckless squirrel would be driven up a detached tree when, if it were not too lofty, he was assailed with clubs and stones, by which (rarely) he would be killed; but more commonly led to jump from its top, when not very high, and run for a taller tree. Such is the sagacity of self preservation—such the knowledge of nature which may be acquired by direct intercourse with her. Throwing at a squirrel or a bird's nest, or to knock down grapes or walnuts, was an admirable exercise for the arm; indeed—for the whole body—and a fine discipline for the eye.

Sometimes the boys brought bows and arrows, and competed for superiority in shooting at a mark. Pitching quoits was a substitute for marble playing. Making whistles in spring out of pawpaw or hickory bark, & blowing on them, was the practice of the fine arts in the midst of our athletic sports. Many of them, like some of which have been named, required equal effort and activity. This was the case with that admirable game, a favorite at all country schools, corner-ball. Running races was another; hop, skip, & jump another; and Prison-base, as Webster calls it, known by us, however, as prisoner's base, was racing in high and complex perfection.

Now, if you contemplate these exercises as performed in

an open and pure air, under embowering trees—festooned with grape vines and choral with little birds, and compare them with the marble playing of city boys on a 'brick pavement, or the feats of a gymnasium with glass windows, hemmed in by big houses, you will admit, I think, that the rural influences are far more propitious to the firm growth of both body and mind, than the civic. It is true that the union of boys and girls within and without a country school house is not free from objections, but it is natural; and if the latter hear some things which they should not, and form some habits not befitting their sex, they become better prepared for the rough and tumble of life, in which the most favoured may be involved. Their constitutions are hardened; & their knowledge of the character of the other sex increased; while the feelings and manners of the boys are to some extent refined by the association.

In all the schools of the period now under review, there was a custom never seen in cities, but still prevalent in remote places, which I highly approve. When the scholars arrived, after the master had taken his seat, the boys were required, on entering the door, to take off their hats and make a bow—the girls to courtesy. In *some* schools, the same was commanded on leaving the house in the evening. But this is not what I just referred to, & to which I now come. It was further inculcated on them to take off their hats and bow and courtesy to all whom they met, either coming or going. Even during play hours, if a man or woman rode near the groups, it was regarded as a duty to give the salutation. Thus I have often run to the roadside with other boys to make my bow; & when a dozen of us or more might be returning together, if a man overtook or met us, we all stepped aside, stopped in a row, took off our hats and made our bows as near as possible at the same time. This was that cultivation of reverence and good manners which, fifty years afterwards, I find so ominously neglected.

Of my progress at this school of voice, manners, and rural sports I can say but little, for after the lapse of 51 or 2 years, I recollect but little. My impression is, that in the matter of *order* I was not a great offender; and I certainly never loitered or played truant. Indeed, I do not remember that I ever perpetrated the latter offense while attending any school. I recollect, however, that I was sometimes flogged or feruled, the summary punishment of those days, and of course had violated some law.

Concerning studies, I took a great deal of pleasure in spelling, and was ranked among the better class of urchins in that acquirement. My first studies in "Cyphering" were here, and my voice and fluency enabled me to "say" the multiplication, in the style of a real declaimer. Of the extent of my penetration into the domain of numbers, I can not speak positively; but think my conquests were limited to addition, multiplication, subtraction, and division, with a few hacks at reduction—all in "round numbers." Of my progress in writing I remember nothing; but of reading, I can speak more positively. Loudness and fluency were my characteristics. Of pronunciation, emphasis, and cadence, or a correct understanding of the subject, I can not boast with the same good conscience. I was fond of getting outside of the house with some other boy, and reading verse about with him in the New Testament. I have at this moment a lively recollection of being thus seated in the afternoon of a bright and pleasant summer day, with the green woods just before us, while we read, with voices which echoed among the leaves, the 5th Chap. of the 1st Epistle to the Thessalonians — remarkable as you are aware for the number of its short verses — the reason, I presume, of my remembering the incident.

I can not tell you how long, by interrupted continuity, *vulgo*, "fits and starts," or, in the commoner dialect of the day, "by spells," I was the pupil of Master Beaden. I think it was through a part of my tenth and perhaps the whole of my 11th year.

My next school master was Kenyon, a Yankee! At that time a *avis rara*, in Kentucky. He was a man of some personal appearance, and, in point of manners, not less than attainments, much superior to Beaden. He taught at the "Lick" in Uncle Cornelius Drakes "still-house." Under him I made some progress. He taught me the "Rule of Three," and I remember to have been puzzled for a day, with the following (poetically expressed) sum:

> "If from a measure three feet high,
>   The Shadow, five is made,
> What is the steeple's height, in yards,
>   That's 90 feet in Shade?"

You'll observe the catch in this. If the *height* of the steeple had been given, to find the *length* of shade, the statement of the case would have been easy. In my perplexity, he declined assisting, and I even doubted whether he could, such was the obscurity with which my obtuseness had invested it, although I was 12 years old! I didn't, however, give it up, and when I was in the woods on my way home in the evening, the truth suddenly flashed upon me. In my joy (as great as that of Archimedes when he discovered a method of detecting the alloy in the crown of the Sicilian monarch) I lost all shame for my **dulness;** and hastening home, boasted to my father and mother of the achievement—which, in their profound ignorance of the subject, they seemed to regard as highly auspicious!

Sometime afterwards, I was confirmed in my suspicion of Kenyon's ignorance; for, continuing to cypher, I reached the "Double rule of Three," and came at length to a sum which *neither* of us could work out. My studies with him were the same in kind as they had been before, but extended in degree. Of grammar, geography & definitions, I presume he knew nothing; still he was of superior scholarship to Beaden. He might have done me considerable good; but in the midst of business he perpetrated a crime and ran away! Here was interruption; but constancy of attendance on school was not my destiny; and, therefore, but little was thought of it.

Sometime afterwards I returned for awhile to the old sylvan Academy, which now had a new Domine——Master *Smith.* I have forgotten his country, but think it was Virginia. He had a son, Charles (with Club foot, who is, or was not long since alive in the same county) with whom I contracted a boy's friendship, and from whom, some years since, I received a letter. Many other companionships also sprung up here. The mother of Dr. Threlkeld, and her brothers, Neel and Jack Waller, the Bassetts, and the Glovers (one of whom, then a small boy, but now an iron founder in this place and a *trustee* of our *University*),[5] were of the number. All were children of poor people, or persons in very moderate circumstances; but these details will not interest you, and I'll stop them.

With Master Smith, I began my classical studies. True, he knew nothing of grammar, etymology, geography, or mathematics; but he had picked up a dozen lines of Latin poetry, which I had an ambition (carried out) to commit to memory. I was much taken with the sounds of the words—the first I had ever heard beyond my native tongue. From the few I now recollect, I presume the quotation was from the eclogues of Virgil. Master Smith changed his locality, and another long vacation ensued.

My next school house was east of Mayslick, but in the edge of the village, about a mile and a quarter from Father's. It was kept in a cabin built by Lawson, a tenant of his while living in the "Lick" and my playground now was, in part, the cucumber patch in which Tom and I stole the cucumbers. I went to this school in winter, and had many a cold tramp through deep snows, which filled my shoes in spite of

[5] Captain William E. Glover (1801-1873), a member of the first Board of Trustees of the University of Louisville. He came to Louisville from Mayslick, Ky., when sixteen years of age and apprenticed himself to a blacksmith. His spare time was devoted to the study of engineering in all its aspects. He was, for a short time, a Captain of an Ohio river steamboat. Later he operated a highly successful foundry and became one of the most prominent men in Louisville.

old stocking legs drawn over them. Of my progress here I cannot recollect anything. I only know that I did not enter on any new study, and that I extended the old a little.

Two incidents, however, remain in my memory, and I will mention them as illustrating my character at that time. A boy by the name of Walter, from mere mischief for we had no quarrel, struck me a hard blow and cut one of my lips, which I did not resent, as most boys would have done; but quietly put up with it. When I went home at night, and was asked the cause of the assault, Father blamed and shamed me for my cowardice. I felt mortified, but was not aroused to any degree of revenge.

The other incident was this. In the open field in which the school house stood, the boys were accustomed to roll great balls of snow, and then dividing themselves into two parties, one was to have possession of the mass, and the other try to take it from them. On one of these occasions, when I belonged to the former battalion, the battle waxed hot enough to melt all the snow in the field. But it was, in fact, a little softened already, and hence our balls were hard and heavy. With these missiles we came to very close quarters, and the small boys, like myself, were sorely pelted on head and face by the larger. However, I never thought of flinching, and if it had come to fists, feet, and teeth, I am quite certain I should have fought until placed *hors de combat* by some overpowering contusion. I am equally certain that the admonition of father did not prompt me on this occasion, in which I was hurt much worse than I should have been in half a dozen ordinary school boy fights.

Now, how are these two displays of character to be

reconciled? They appear to stand in direct opposition. As they involve principles which have run through my whole life, I will offer you my speculations concerning them. Naturally, I took no pleasure in witnessing a combat of any kind—not even that of dogs or game cocks, the fights of which were, in those days, common *amusements*. The fights of men, which I often saw, also affected me unpleasantly. Thus, I had not a pugnacious temper. Again, I was rather "slow to anger," that is, to the point of resentment. Again, mother had taught me to regard fighting as wicked, and had not established in my mind any distinction between fighting in aggression and fighting in defense. She was, *in extenso*, a *non combatant*. Finally, when not adequately aroused, I was **timmed,** and the aggressions which are so often productive of fights among boys did not arouse me. The opposite emotion counteracted my anger. In the snow-balling, my ambition, not my anger, was up. I was under an adequate motive, one which excited me, and no fear or thought of personal danger came into my mind. I will illustrate this subject by an incident which occurred about 4 years afterwards in the early period of my studies with Dr Goforth. I had a fellow student and two boys from a neighbouring town were boarding and lodging at the Doctor's, to go to school. The older & larger, corresponding to me in age & size, offered me various insults, and spoke against me behind my back, but at the time of giving the insults I did not resent them. At length, one morning, when the other two had gone down stairs, and we were partly dressed (for we all lodged in the same room) it came into my mind and heart to whip him, although he had not then said a word to me. So at it we went, and in half a minute he cried out enough!—a cry which I should not have uttered by the next morning. Still he would have fought, at any time, under a provocation which would not have moved me to retaliation but, perhaps, made me afraid.

But I must return to the school house where I shall not detain you long. The teacher's name was Kneeland, and he also, was a yankee. He soon afterwards "put off," but under what opprobrium I do not now remember.

My next and last tutor before commencing the study of medicine, was my old Master Smith, who now *ruled* the boys and girls in another log school house, under a great shell bark hickory among the haw trees, on the banks of the *Shannon,* about two miles West of father's. To him I was sent, more or less, through the spring, summer, & early autumn of the year 1800, when I was in my 15th year. As my destiny to the profession of medicine was now a "fixed fact," I was taking the finishing touches; and yet spelling, reading, writing, and cyphering constituted the *curriculum* of Master Smith's college.

Among my school mates were many of my old companions, and many new ones, including the family of Gen. Desha,[6] afterwards Governor of Kentucky. His son, who murdered Baker in 1823, between the Blue Licks and Mays Lick, that he might get his horse and saddle, was one of them. His brother, now Gen. Robert Desha[7] of Mobile, a

[6] General Joseph Desha (1768-1842), served as a Major General at the battle of the Thames, as a Member of the Kentucky Legislature, Member of Congress (1807-1819), and Governor of Kentucky (1824-1828).

[7] General Robert Desha (1770?-1849), soldier, Congressman from Tennessee (1827-1831), and later a merchant in Mobile, Alabama.

former brother in law of Dr. Fearn, and a gentleman whom you saw in Nashville, and afterwards in Gallatin, Tenn., was another. He, as far as I know, of all my school fellows, then or before, is the only one who has attained any distinction in society. Judge McLean's father, however, once resided in Mayslick a little while, when I was about 7 or 8 years old, and the judge[8] and myself might then have gone to the same school. I have never thought to ask him. When I went to Master Smith the second time, I felt more than I had ever done before, the necessity of application. I felt anxious concerning the future, knew that my deficiencies were great, and really sought to make the most of my time.

A.M. ½ past 12. From 2 P.M. till 10, I wrote the preceding 20 pages. I had then to prepare for Mrs Prof^r Caldwell's Drawing room, which I reached a quarter before 11 & left a quarter after 12, meeting a gentleman and lady going in as I came out. It was a sore affliction for me to feel obliged to stop, however much you may be relieved by it.

You might ask, *how* I could know of deficiencies in my preparation for the study of a science of which I was so ignorant? My answer is at hand, and will involve a notice of my cousin

Dr. John Drake

He was the younger son of Uncle Abraham Drake, the *tavern keeper, merchant* and rich man of the family. John

[8] John McLean (1785-1861), jurist, Member of Congress, Postmaster General (1823-1829), Associate Justice of the United States Supreme Court (1830).

was 5, 6 or 7 years older than myself. When I was 4 or 5, he used to excite my wonder and that of the other children, with stories of Jack the Giant Killer, Bluebeard, & other great men, for which he had a remarkable talent. From the number of his Classical books, now in my possession, I infer that he had been sent to school in Washington, [Ky.], to some good scholar who *might* have been there. He went to the study of medicine in that town with Dr Goforth, about the year 1795 or 6. His progress as a medical student was rapid. His talents were various. In the Thespian Corps he maintained a high rank, and in the debating society, his eloquence was enviable. In manners he attained to ease and grace. His person was rather small and delicate, but his presence, I well recollect, was highly prepossessing. In the autumn of 1798 or 9, he went to Phil^a to attend lectures, and when I did the same thing in the Fall of 1805, and wrote my name on P^rof Barton's[9] Register, he immediately inquired after my namesake, and spoke of him in high terms. That the *professor* should have remembered him so long depressed my spirits, for I felt how greatly behind him I must be; seeing that the idea of being thus remembered could not be entertained by me for a moment. John spent the spring and summer at home in Mayslick with his father, diligently pursuing his studies, and, I believe, adding the Latin Language to the Medical Sciences. He was to attend

[9] Benjamin Smith Barton (1766-1815), often called "the father of American materia medica," was professor of this subject in the Medical Department of the University of Pennsylvania from 1796 to 1813. He was then elected to the Professorship of the Practice of Medicine made vacant by the death (1813) of Benjamin Rush.

lectures the following winter, and then establish himself in Mayslick, *when I was to become his pupil.* Now it was from him, in various conversations, and from looking into his Classical and Medical books, that I came to an apprehension of my inadequate preparation for the enterprise on which I was about to enter. His constitution was frail, and in the month of July he was seized with a slow fever of the typhous kind. The physicians of Washington, Drs Johnson & Duke, attended him; but he gradually got worse. At length his father, who doted on him, despatched our Cousin Jacob Drake to Cincinnati for Dr Goforth. The D^r could not come, and about the time Jacob got back, riding all night, through a tremendous and awful thunder storm, with some advice in his pocket, John expired [August 7, 1800.] His remains now repose in the old village Church yard. A young man of the brightest genius and the noblest qualities of heart, he would have conferred distinction on our name and his memory should be transmitted in the family. All his books & manuscript notes came & remain in my possession.

Had he lived, I should not have gone to Cincinnati to study medicine, and of a consequence, never resided there. In fact, humanly speaking, my whole course of life might have been entirely different from what it has been. I should probably have become a country Doctor and a member of the General Assembly! His death did not turn my father aside from the determination that I should study physic. I still continued to make my way daily through two miles of woods to the log school house on the banks of the Shannon. We had, moreover, a great deal of work to do on the farm, and I felt that as I was not only soon to leave father, but become an expense to him, I ought to tax myself to the utmost. Thus I rose early, and worked in the field till breakfast time, and after that, very commonly *ran* the two miles, to be in time. But my health was good, my endurance great, and we always retired early at night.

In the midst of this last effort, however, a family affliction arose, which greatly interrupted my studies. Father got a severe injury on his foot, which partially mortified, and three or four of the children were taken down with the ague & fever, the first time that that disease had ever invaded us. In my letter two years ago, I must have mentioned these facts, but probably did not tell you (boastingly) that when the care of *every* thing turned on mother and myself, my heart grew big with the emotions which such calamities naturally inspire. The feeling of responsibility that was quite as natural produced in my actions their proper fruits. Father and mother commended me for my labours, both in doors & out. To speak of the whole matter frankly, I look back, even from this distant point of time, 47 years, to my conduct with approbation and pleasure. What a precious reward (referring to this life only) there is in striving to do what trying occasions require of us. As old age is ruminant, youth ought to prepare for it as many savory cuds as possible.

Well! I have given you an unpremeditated and unbroken, though very imperfect, narrative of my opportunities for *scholastic* learning before I commenced the study of medicine. I had some, of a collateral and incidental kind, to

which, I must refer. It is, however, nearly 2 o'c'k A.M. &
therefore, I'll say—*good night*.

Jan. 14ᵗʰ P.M. During my boyhood, there was in the
country (except among wealthy emigrants from Old
Virginia of whom, however, there were none about Mayslick) a great deficiency of books. There was not a single
book store north of Licking River and, perhaps, none in the
state. All the books imported were kept in what were called
Stores, which were magazines of the most primitive
character—variety shops, if not curiosity shops— compre-
hending dry goods, hardware, glass & earthen ware,
groceries, dyestuffs & drugs, **amunition,** hats, manufactures
of leather, books, and stationery—the last consisting generally of coarse fools cap, wafers, slates & pencils. The era of
division of labour and distribution of commodities on sale,
had not yet arrived. Of course no particular branch was
pushed very far; and least of all, that which ministered to
intellectual improvement, for its articles were least in
demand. Bibles, hymn books, primers, spelling books, arith-
metics & almanacs, in fact composed, in most instances, the
importation, which was always from Phil[a]—the only City of
the seaboard which maintained any commercial intercourse
with the infant settlements of the interior.

Our preachers and teachers were, in general, almost as
destitute as the people at large, many of whom could
neither read nor write, did not send their children to school,
and of course, kept no books in the house. Of our own
library I have already spoken incidentally. A family Bible,
Rippon's Hymns, Watts' hymns for children, the Pilgrims

progress, an old Romance of the days of Knight Errantry, primers, with a plate representing John Rogers[10] at the stake, spelling books, an arithmetic & a new almanac for the new year, composed all that I can recollect, till within 2 or 3 years of my leaving home. Now, comparing myself with other boys of my age, I think I had a taste for study rather greater than the bulk of them, and if books had been within my reach, it is probable that I should have made some proficiency by solitary study at night and on rainy days.

When I was about 12 or 13 years old, Father purchased of a neighbour living a mile down *Absalom,* a copy of Love's Surveying,[11] which I well remember afforded me great pleasure. Its definitions and diagrams—triangles, trapeziums & Rhomboids—now come up pleasantly in the vista through which I am reviewing the past. I even went so far as to plat tracts of land according to courses & distances. But I was not a young **Paschal**. I had a taste rather than a talent for Geometry, and did not go on "conquering and to conquer." Ten years afterwards, however, the propensity to that science recurred, and finding Euclid's Elements among the books which had belonged to Cousin John Drake, I put

[10] John Rogers (1500?-1555), English clergyman and martyr, an intimate of Tyndale for whom he made marginal notes and prepared for publication his version of the Bible. Rogers was thrown into prison for preaching against popery, and sentenced to death as a heretic. He was the first of the ninety-six Protestants executed in 1555 by Mary I, Queen of England.

[11] John Love, an Englishman, author of *Geodaesia: or the Art of Surveying, and Measuring Land Made Easy* ... This was a popular textbook of the late seventeenth and eighteenth centuries which went through more than a dozen editions.

at them, but stopped again after I had solved the 47th proposition; being delighted to observe that it was by a rule dependent on that problem that I had, with others, squared the Corners of small cabins and outhouses while I was on the farm. My capacity for Arithmetic was, I suppose, up to the mean heat, for before I went from home I had learned decimals & vulgar fractions, gauging, Position, and *heard* of Algebra. Many years afterwards curiosity prompted me to look a little into that Science, but I found it rather hard, & not so much to my taste as Geometry, and stopped, after going through the Binomial Theorem. Limited and superficial as were these dippings into mathematical science, they have not been without their value, for they taught me what the objects and (to some small extent) the processes of that science are. [They] enabled me to understand some things in my studies which would otherwise have been unintelligible.

Another book which fell into my hands (I can not tell how) when I was 12 or 13, was Guthrie's Grammar of Geography,[12] the study of which was undoubtedly of service; though, as it was not intended for children, much of it was beyond my comprehension. Its hard technical terms pestered me a great deal, not only as to their meaning, but their pronunciation. The phrase, "Brazen Meridian" which I ejaculated with a strong accent on the penultimate, was one of those *posers*. The very title of that book puzzled

12 William Guthrie (1708-1770), English schoolmaster and, later the author of historical, political and geographical works. Of Guthrie, Dr. Samuel Johnson said to Boswell, "Sir, he is a man of parts. He has no great regular fund of knowledge; but by reading so long, and writing so long, he no doubt has picked up a great deal."

me, for I had read in the spelling book that grammar related to words, and I could not, therefore, understand its connection with a description of the earth. My first crude ideas of latitude and longitude, of the equator and the rotundity of the earth, were derived from the study of this work. We had, in the family, a tradition that our great namesake Sir Francis Drake (possibly we were relations) was the first man who sailed *round* the world. I had long been perplexed to know how that could be, but now understood it. An old hunter who visited at Father's had spoken of the *noction* line. I saw in Guthrie that it was *equinoctial,* and could laugh at his ignorance. I feel grateful to Mr Guthrie for his patient teachings of so dull a pupil, and would like to meet with him again.

Before I fell in with the grammar of Geography, I was advanced from Dilworth's to Webster's spelling book. I was greatly interested in its augmented vocabulary of new & hard words, and in the new reading it afforded, especially in the account of the boy who pronounced to his father an opinion in favour of the superior pleasures of each of the four seasons, as they successively arose. I was in sympathy with him, and *now* know that I then had, in a *germinal* state, a trait of character which, in expansion, has remained with me ever since. It is an aptitude to become interested in *every* thing — in *any* study or *any* pursuit, and to derive from it as much pleasure, *pro tempore,* as from any other.

A couple of years, or thereabouts, before leaving home, I got Entick's (a pocket) dictionary which was, of course a great acquisition. I also obtained Scott's Lessons, which afforded me much new reading, and I used to "speak" pieces from it at Master Smith's school, when I went to him the second time. In addition (but not to my school library), father purchased I remember (when I was 12 or 13) the Prompter, Esop's Fables, & Franklin's Life—all sterling books for boys. The first was a collection of proverbs and maxims. A puzzle growing out of the last was his being called doctor, when he had not studied physic!

Occasionally, father borrowed books for me of Dr Goforth. Once he bought me the Farmer's Letters, a work by Dickinson, Secretary to Congress during the Revolutionary War. Much of it was above my comprehension, but it made the mind strain forward—an effect produced about the same time by Guthrie's Grammar.

Another book from the same source, borrowed, I think, a year or so earlier when I was 11 or 12, was Lord Chesterfield's Letters to his son, inculcating politeness. This fell in mighty close with my tastes, and not less with those of father and mother, who cherished as high and pure an idea of the duty of good breeding as any people on earth. The principle of politeness was deeply rooted in both. Their manifestation of it, in the form of deference, in their way, was sometimes, as I thought (even at that early period) carried too far. I was always, however, prone to be deferential, and was never inclined or able, to act with rudeness or *non chalance* in the presence of my Seniors or superiors. Time, of which the elements are observation & reflection, has convinced me that our natural deference ought to be cherished & that we should cultivate a feeling of respect for what is respectable, while we manifest suavity and kindness to all.

In the olden time newspapers, now the cumbersome pests of so many families, were almost as scarce among the country people around us as Sibylline leaves, and no *tracts* were spoken of in the house, but those of land. The first newspaper published in the state of Kentucky was begun at Lexington in 1787, the year before our immigration. It was called the Kentucky Gazette[13] and edited, printed and published by John Bradford. Another was started in Washington, when I was 8 or 9 years old; but Father did not take it. It was called the Palladium.[14] Occasionally a number of it fell into my hands and was, from its novelty and variety, a great treat, although much of it was, of course, unintelligible. It spoke I remember, a great deal about the French Revolution, Bonaparte & the war between France and England; in reference to which Father and his neighbours were in close sympathy with the French. I recollect getting a number of it when I was about 11 years old. It was soon after corn planting, and I was sent into the cornfield to keep out the squirrels. I took the paper with me, and leaving the young corn to defend itself as it could, sat down at the root

[13] Dr. Drake is not entirely correct because *The Kentucke Gazette*, as it was first known, was established Aug. 11, 1787 *jointly* by John and Fielding Bradford. The name of the paper was changed to *The Kentucky Gazette* in 1789 and its publication was continued by John Bradford until 1802 when he transferred it to his son, Daniel.

[14] This is an error. *The Palladium: a Literary and Political Weekly Repository* was established at Frankfort, Ky., in 1798. The publishers of *The Palladium* had established *The Mirror* at Washington, Ky., in 1797. The fact that these two papers were published simultaneously by the same firm may account for Dr. Drake's mistake.

of a large tree near the center of the little field (where of course the squirrels would not disturb me) and, beginning at the head of the first column, on the first page, read it through – advertisements and all. This may seem to you rather laughable, but it was all right (the neglect of the corn excepted) for it gave me a peep into the world & excited my curiosity.

And now, my dear Dove, I have given you as full a detail as memory permits of my scholastic opportunities, and home studies. If I add anything to my narrative, it must be drawing on my imagination, as others have done who are the heroes of their own histories. This brings to my recollection that the Life of Robinson Crusoe (greatest of Autobiographers) was among my early readings. I have not read it for 45 or 50 years, but long and often *threaten* to do it yet. I neglect to hunt it up, and it never falls in my way. From the size, it must have been an abridgment that I read in days of yore; but it was so well executed that the whole was to me a living reality. So it appears, I presume, to other children; for I remember that when your brother was about 11 years of age, he came in one evening in a great flurry, and told his mother and myself that he had just seen Robinson Crusoe down in Broadway. I asked how he knew it was Robinson, & he said because he was dressed in skins; getting his copy, at the same time, & showing me a frontispiece which represented the hero in that costume. I then told him that the life was a mere tale – a story – and not a true account; but he could not believe me, and gave as a reason that there was so *much of it*. Thus it is, that circumstantiality, under the hand of genius, leads to irresistible conviction. In common with other children, I experienced in my boyhood all this, when reading the Pilgrim's progress. Although it was declared to be a dream, all the characters became to me as real personages — as real as if they had been dramatis personae acting before me.

By an association of ideas which I can not understand, I am now reminded of a very *wee* book, the title of which does not come up with the story. It told of two children, a brother and sister, being in captivity somewhere in Eastern Africa or Arabia, and after a long separation, being brought accidentally together and lodged in the same bed, with a man between them; and how they pressed and locked each other's hands over his body. The effect on my feelings (I well remember) was so agonizing, as to indicate not only great intensity of fraternal love and tenderness, but an apt personation of character by me. The latter has remained with me ever since, and is one reason why all works of fiction raise in me emotions so powerful that I am obliged, in a great degree, to avoid their perusal.

Father, as well as myself, was aware that I was about to go to the study of medicine without due scholastic preparation. If there had been a classical School in our neighbourhood, I should, no doubt, have been sent to it, for some months at least. Under the conviction which I have assigned to him, he stipulated with Dr Goforth that I should be sent to school for six months, to learn Latin. By some great absurdity this was not done till I had studied for 18 mo. that which, for want of Latin, I could not understand. But to dwell on this would be foreign to my present object. In making a deliberate and, as far as might be expected, a candid estimate of my natural and acquired preparation for the study and practice of medicine, I am led to the conclusion, that both kinds of qualification were more in the moral than the intellectual elements of my character.

I was free from *gross* vices, or even a tendency to them, and was protected by *some* degree of conscientiousness. I was still further defended by a love of approbation and praise, which was far from being either dilute or easily cloyed; but I was not made vain, self conceited, or a "spoiled child" by its administration. On the contrary, the pleasure it afforded was mingled with humility and a kind of regret that I did not deserve more of the same savory aliment of the soul, and a renewed resolution to earn additional supplies by greater exertions in line of duty. This was a salutary effect of commendation, and indicated a low state of pride. That passion was, indeed, never strong; and, moreover, was counterpoised by a humility which always suggested how far short I came of the excellence which ought to be attained. With these traits, if I had been born a slave, I should never have become a rebel, but conforming to my condition, rendering diligent service, have acquired the confidence of my master. I had patience without apathy, and endurance without insensibility. My curiosity was keen, & my desire for knowledge much stronger than my consciousness of a capacity for acquiring it. I thought how pleasant it would be to know a great deal; but durst not hope that my talents would procure for me the gratification. I had an idea that those who had studied science deeply, and written books, or become otherwise distinguished, had not only been favoured with greater opportunities, but far greater talents than myself.

As to my actual attainments in learning, they were certainly quite limited, & yet I could read & examine a dictionary for the meaning of words, & here is the starting point of all improvement. My intellectual preparation consisted less, perhaps, in my actual scholarship, than in the want of those habits of sustained application and that strength of memory, which (in ordinary minds) can only be acquired in boyhood. I had, it is true, an ability to engage readily in any study, but at the same time, might be easily diverted from it to any other. I had not been disciplined into the constancy of attention which it is an office of the school master to establish within the walls of the school, where nature, *my* greatest teacher, is shut out. Now, as nature teaches by the works and events which, in the embodiment, constitute the best definition of the word itself, it follows, from her complex character, that her pupils are instructed in many things at the same time or in quick succession. Although the faculty of observation, from continued exercise, may acquire much strength, the attention is not drilled into concentrated protracted devotion to one subject. It results, then ,from all I have said, that when I engaged in the study of medicine, I had a natural and acquired preparation to become a useful physician, but not to enlarge the boundaries of medical science, by the discoveries & inventions of genius.

And now, my dear Dove, I have written you (through yesterday afternoon, & that of today) — (it is now 9 o'c'k) a very long letter—longer than that to any other member of the family (though not elongated thro' design), a longer letter than you ever received before, or will ever receive again. Yet, a number of things which I expected to put into it have not been reached. An old man's pen, once turned upon the days of his youth, is a siphon, with one end in the great reservoir of the past, and the other on his paper, through which the current *will* flow on till the vessel is exhausted.

That you, at my age may have as *good* children, to receive the outpourings of your reminiscential hours, is the prayer of your affectionate

Father

OBSERVATIONS AND ANECDOTES

THE SETTING

There are fourteen paragraphs in the following letter which were omitted from the 1870 Edition. The deleted material was essentially philosophical and, perhaps, controversial. Charles D. Drake, in this emasculation of his father's manuscript, plainly showed the deliberate intention of concealing opinions, when either controversial or derogatory. C. D. D. may have regarded his father as somewhat heretical in believing superstition (that which is spiritual and beyond human understanding) synonymous with religious faith.

Letter Eight

OBSERVATIONS AND ANECDOTES

To Mrs. James Parker Campbell[1]

> Louisville, [Kentucky]
> Jany 14th, 1848
> Friday, 10 o'c'k P.M.

My dear Harriet,

    After finishing (half an hour since) a letter of 35 pages to Bettie, I concluded to allay the thirst occasioned by some of Virginia's excellent, supper table ham, by eating an apple. Having done so, I have taken up one of brother Charles' equally excellent new pens, and begun a letter to you. The *commencement* of it is in full view before me, while the end is too distant, or, more properly speaking, too enveloped in the mists & clouds of futurity, to be seen.

    My letter to "sister Margaret," spoke of maternal and household influences—that to "sister Belle," of forest influences—that to sister Bettie, of scholastic influences—& this is intended to set forth religious and social influences, and all other influences which may occur to me as having been efficiently operative on my character in boyhood;— especially during the six years which elapsed between the

---

[1] Younger daughter of Dr. Drake, Mrs. James Parker Campbell, to whom Letter I was addressed.

time of our removal into the woods and my departure for Cin. Look out, then, for a medley, and be patient, persevering & resigned. In announcing my topics, I put religious before social, but have already changed my mind, & resolved to transpose them.

My letter to "sister Belle" began with Society, but I soon wandered into the woods. I must now come to the point from which we departed. None of those who have lived where they saw many persons every hour in the day, can fully estimate the feeling of loneliness which comes into the heart when only trees and a few domestic animals can be seen. This feeling was ours, and especially mother's, for the first year or two after we left the young but somewhat stirring village (so fully presented to you in my last), for the seclusion of our "new home." A day would often pass without our seeing any one, while before our removal we saw many every hour. Moreover, we no longer saw the great wagons, laden with merchandise for the interior; the caravans of travelers, mounted on horseback; and the gangs of negroes on foot—all moving on to the south. This solitude, however painful (as it was) at the time, had its advantages. It drew us more closely together, and compelled us to rely more intimately on each other. It enabled us to extract from the visits & company we *did* have, a high degree of enjoyment. I well recollect that when anybody came, I was all the time afraid he was about to start away. The coming of a negro on an errand was a welcome event, and the visit of a boy, even on business, was a matter of delight. My social aptitudes and affections were, indeed, quite as strong at that time as they have remained ever since. (Although it's only 11 o'clock, I am, as my two pages have shown you, very *dull* — so *Good night.*)

Saturday P.M. An hour or two since, I finished my lecture, and the supplementary duty of prescribing for some half a dozen invalid students (a duty which I am generally called upon to perform daily). I was about to say, I should have nothing official to do, till 11 A.M., on Monday, when I recollected the stated meeting of our Phy. Temp. Society tonight, at which I have to lecture on *Mania à potu.* Thus, you see, that if in the days of boyhood, I was, as set forth in my letter to James, a dealer in whiskey, I am, in those of old age, not a rectifier of that poison, but of the perverted taste which abuses it, and of my own perverted employments in boyhood. It is curious and lamentable to observe how much of our time in later life is necessarily devoted, or ought to be, to the correction of the effects of the mistakes and errors of youth. This, however, is not the kind of moralizing which was in my mind when I took up my pen. *That* was suggested by the latter part of what I wrote last night.

It is a beautiful law of human nature, that things which act upon us but seldom should produce much more effect than those which act constantly; or, rather, that the *same* influence in occasional application, should, in the end, do as much, as if applied constantly. During its absence our sensibility to it becomes accumulated, and, of course, its impression is more vividly felt.

At Mayslick, our social enjoyments were not neglected,

but we were unconscious of them. In the woods, we felt their interruption, and we also felt their return. There is something in this periodical reproduction of an emotion — in the alternate presence and absence of a social stimulant that may, on the whole, I think, be regarded as salutary to character. I am inclined to think that it tends to exalt our sensibilities; and it certainly tends to equalize the enjoyments of our race. In a former letter I have probably referred to this law of human nature in its application to our bodies — I now speak of it in reference to our minds. Deprivation, then, when not carried too far or continued too long, compensates itself. In pursuance of this idea I would say, the family happiness of the whole of *us* is not diminished by my sojourn in Louisville; though it *would* be, by a permanent removal hither; for that would carry deprivation beyond the proper degree.

I have given you to understand that *any* kind of company was acceptable to us. *Our* desire was for *society*, as the desire of a *hungry* family is for food — or of one suffering from *cold* for *clothes*. In those early times, when many families depended on the woods for meat, they preferred venison or turkey, but if the father returned from hunting without game of any kind, his trophies, on the next return, were hailed with joy, although they might consist of nothing better than 'possums or the ribs of a bear. Again, they might prefer linsey-woolsey for coats and round-abouts, but at a certain point of suffering from cold, would rejoice in deer skins — dressed or undressed. Thus there is a point of intensity of desire at which we cease to discriminate, and gratefully accept whatever belongs to the class of objects on which the desire is directed. I make these rather commonplace remarks in self defense, or more properly, in family defense, that you may not suppose our social tastes utterly undiscriminating and deficient in refinement when, in fact, they were more fastidious than those of the generality of our neighbours. But, for the first two years of our *country* residence, we were kept all the time near the point of social bereavement, at which all fastidiousness disappears; a new condition to all of us. Father and mother emigrated from a densely settled part of N. Jersey, and had passed through the stirring scenes of the Revolution, in which their native state so largely participated. I and my sisters, as I have already shown you, had from our earliest recollections, seen "much people" in Mayslick. Had our visitors, however, been so numerous as to prompt and permit selection, we should have had no great range of choice; and this brings me to say something of our neighbours.

Mays Lick, as I told you in my former letter, was a colony of East Jersey people, amounting in the aggregate to 52 souls.[2] Mr Tenant, who married aunt Lydia, was a West Jersey-man, & he settled near the great road 2 miles from us. Jonathan Stout & Abraham Stout and William Dye, each of whom lived within a mile, were all from the same part of that state. William Johnson, or "old Billy" as he was familiarly called, who had married father's Cousin, though last from Virginia, was originally from Jersey. The Hickson's, two families, who resided near uncle Tenant's, the Bunnells & Cahills, were also from that state. Thus, I

[2] The present (1947) population of Mayslick is 350.

have enumerated 13 families, and think there were more. The immigrants from other states were almost entirely Virginians and Marylanders. All were country people by birth and residence — all were illiterate, but in various degrees — & all were poor, or in moderate circumstances — a majority or, at least, a moiety, however, were small freeholders.

As to religious and moral refinement & a knowledge and use of the domestic arts of civilized life, the Jersey emigrants, as a body, were superior. Next came the Virginians, and last and lowest, the Marylanders; who, in many respects, were not equal to the Kentucky negroes of the *present* day. Of such was my old *domine,* Master Beaden.

The Jersey people were generally without slaves, partly from principle, and partly from the want of means. Most of the settlers from Virginia and Maryland brought slaves with them, though the number in each family was small — often one only. Consequently, these families had to work, though not to the same extent as those from Jersey & a few scattered here and there from other states, where slaves were few in number.

The mechanic arts practiced at that time were only those which are inseparable from civilization. The blacksmith, house carpenter, turner, tanner, shoemaker, tailor, weaver, and such like, made the whole, and all were very common-place in skill. The great occupation was clearing off the forest and cultivating the rich & fresh new soil, which **reveled** in the sunshine; of which, from April to November, through an indefinite period of time, it had been deprived by the overshadowing woods. The little clearings with

their log cabins were detached from each other by intervening forest, through which foot paths, bridle paths, and
narrow wagon roads, obstructed with stumps, wound their
way. Although several families might live within the sound
of a rifle or a falling bee tree, a boy felt himself in the almost
unbroken wilderness, raising in him an exaggerated idea
of the distance from place to place; as I was deeply convinced, on my last visit in 1845 to the same neighbourhood,
when so much of the forest had been destroyed as to bring
places, which 55 years before had seemed quite remote,
into full view of each other, and make them seem quite near.

It is a remarkable fact that in the early period of which
I am writing, from 1794 to 1800, the white population was
greater in that neighbourhood than I found it in the visit
referred to. In a single, solitary walk of two miles, which
included the spot of our old home, I passed over the
foundations — the decayed logs and dust, of no less than 12
cabins, on the broad hearths of which I used to warm myself
in winter, or play around in other seasons, when sent on
errands, or permitted to visit the boys and girls with which
they were redolent. Besides, I saw two of a better kind than
the first, erected of hewed (hewn) logs, which were tenant-
less and surrounded by hemp. Their inmates might almost
be said to have perished by the hemp. One of these was that
which my father had built after I left home, and behind
which he had, by rebuilding, placed as a kitchen our
primitive cabin, on the logs and door cheeks of which I
found the rude figures and initials I had inscribed with my
Barlow pen knife, 50 years before. Weeds & briers were
growing round the door; and an unutterable feeling of awe

& melancholy came over me, as I trod upon the sill on which
I used to sit with my little sisters and brothers, to be pushed
aside by our dear mother, as she went in and out, on her
quiet and willing daily duties. Of the whole family, eight in
number, one besides myself remained, to visit and commune with the abandoned & desolate friend of our
childhood.

The loss of white population, so impressively shown
forth by what I have said, has occurred in various parts of
Kentucky, and must be referred to the influence of slavery.
As bodies of different specific gravity rise to the surface in
different times, so in every community, some will rise in the
world more rapidly than others. In a slave state, new
investments are constantly made in land and negroes, and
hence the soil is constantly passing from the many to
the few. Slaves take the place of freemen, "negro quarters"
replace the humble habitations of happy families. He who
had a stirring and laborious father rides over the augmented
plantation as a lord, and the hired man with his axe or sickle
is replaced by the overseer with his thong.

But you must return to the primitive settlement, and
meditate on the social circumstances under which I passed
what I suppose, in reference to the formation of character,
to have been the most important period in my life — that in
which it got its "set." To aid you in the estimate of influences, I must give you some details. Immigrants into the
wilderness are, or rather become, social and hospitable;
for their insulation makes them glad to see each other. They
have private or family visiting, with abundance of small
talk about the countries they had left, about their pursuits,

their children, and *their neighbours,* in the last of which, according to my experience, they do not yield to people under any other circumstance. They also have many gatherings. Some are composed of men and boys only, for raising houses, stables & barns, for rolling logs, for husking corn, for opening new roads, and other purposes; all of which I have repeatedly attended, and well recollect that profanity, vulgarity & drinking were their most eminent characteristics. *All* drank, though not to excess, but all of course did not participate in other vices, yet I am bound to say that coarse jocularities were scarcely frowned upon by any. Some sort of physical amusement, including fights, in which biting & gouging were essential elements, with the beastly intoxication of several, would generally "wind up" these meetings.

(P.M. 9-½ o'c'k. A little after 6, I broke off to go to supper, and thence to the meeting of the Phy. Temp. Society. The Society was in session 2 hours, an hour and a half of which was occupied with my lecture. I got back a few minutes since, and have just attempted to tranquillize my nerves with a piece of gingerbread from the Bakery of Campbell, Graham & Co.,[3] together with a glass of water.)

That I was preserved from any active participation in or permanent contamination from, these associations to which I can trace up the ruin of many of my companions, ought to fill my heart with gratitude to God. The influences, under Him, which protected me were, I think, in part, my natural

3 Playful reference to his children.

tastes & feelings, but in greater part, the admonition of my parents, and of mother still more perhaps than Father.

> Blest is the heedless little boy
>   To whom is given,
>   (The boon of Heaven)
> A pious mother, ever kind,
> Yet never to his wand'rings blind:
>
> Who watches every erring step
>   In holy fear,
>   And drops a tear
> Of pity on the chast'ning Rod,
> Then strikes, and points, in prayer, to God.

We had other gatherings composed of females only, or of the two sexes united. Dances were not common, I was never present at one. Weddings, commonly in the day time were scenes of carousal, and of mirth and merriment of no very chastened character. The "infare" of the following day presented on the winding road through the green woods a long and picturesque cavalcade, in which the cavalier and his "lady love" were paired off with the groom and bride in the van. At the house of *his* father the scenes of the preceding day were re-enacted, with such new accompaniments as new members of the company could suggest, or the inventions of a night of excited genius had brought forth.

Another kind of gathering was the quilting party. Towards evening the young men would assemble, and amuse themselves by athletic exercises without, or talking to, and "plaguing the gaals" within the cabin. The quilt being removed, the supper table took its place, and after the ladies had risen from the "cream" of the feast, the gentlemen, who had whetted their appetites by drinking whiskey and looking on, proceeded to glut themselves on the *reliquiae*. Then came on plays of various kinds, interlarded with jokes and bursts of laughter, till bed time, when the dispersion took place.

At other times, small parties were made up by invitation, which were, of course, more select and conducted with greater decorum. If on a "week day," they were generally in the evening, for the men had to work in the day time; but on Sunday, they began in the afternoon. Among the most pious, Sunday, after worship, was regarded as a fit time for visiting, even in considerable parties. They were, however, conducted with greater propriety, and hymns and spiritual songs often made a part of the entertainment. Sunday was also the time for the visits of the young people, especially of young gentlemen from Washington, many of whom sought our community for amusement, & to be among those whose lower rank would allow them wide latitude of manners and conduct.

Up to the time of my leaving home, I was too young to participate much in what I have described. On my visits during my pupilage, I was an occasional participant, and at all times an attentive observer. When not 12 years old, I saw much at which my taste and moral sense revolted, and father and mother strengthened me in the aversion. On a calm survey in retrospect of the whole community, I am compelled to say that in purity & refinement, it did not rank high. I doubt the correctness of what is sometimes said in favour of country life among the labouring classes; and lean to the opinion, that city people of a corresponding grade as to intelligence, property, and pursuits, have, on the whole, more virtue and chaster manners. *Adieu.*

Sunday 2 P.M.[4] As I am writing on morals, in this particular part of what I fear you will regard as a very long letter, I hope it will not be thought by you against the sanctity of the Sabbath, especially when I tell you that I shall not allow it to limit my usual attendance on the duties of the Sanctuary, which I have visited twice today, and expect to enter a third time tonight.

What I have said on the preceding pages, will show you, on what models my observance of the Sabbath was formed. I find constant evidence, in my recollections and present consciousness, that the germs of my opinion relative to the Sabbath were implanted at the time of which I have been writing. Suspension of labour & attendance on public worship were required but social enjoyments were not forbidden; hence, my taste for them on that day, is strong down to the present time.

The Baptists, of which were my parents, many of my relatives, and a majority of our religious friends were never as strict observers of the Sabbath as the Presbyterians. I often heard my father say that he had known men belonging to that connexion who would sit up stiff and holy the whole of Sunday, and on Monday, would curse & swear.

[4] The following four paragraphs were not inserted in the 1870 edition of this book.

But I have taken a different path from that which I intended to follow, and must turn back to the "forks of the road." Having done so, let me conduct you to the village from which I led you in my 1st letter.

Mays Lick

This place, although scarcely a village, was once an emporium and capital for a tract of country 6 or 8 miles in diameter, embracing several hundred families, of which those in father's neighbourhood were tolerably fair specimens. Uncle Abr. Drake kept a store, and Shotwell & Morris kept taverns; besides them there were a few poor mechanics. Uncle Cornelius Drake was a farmer merely, and lived a little out of the center of the station, the great men of which were the three I have just named. With this limited population it, even down to this time, seems wonderful to me that such gatherings and such scenes should have been transacted there. They commenced within 5 years after its settlement, and increasing with the progress of surrounding population, continued in full vigour long after I left home for Cincinnati. It was *the* place for holding Regimental militia musters, when all the boys and old men of the surrounding country, not less than those who stood enrolled, would assemble. Before dispersing at night, the training was quite eclipsed by a heterogeneous drama of foot racing, pony racing, wrestling, fighting, drunkenness and general uproar.

It was also a place for political meetings and stump conflict by opposing candidates, & after intellectual performances there generally followed an epilogue of oaths, yells, loud blows, & gnashing of teeth.

Singing schools were likewise held at the same place in a room of Deacon Morris' tavern. I was never a scholar, which I regret, for it has always been a grief with me that I did not learn music in early life. I occasionally attended. As in all country singing schools, sacred music only was taught but, in general, there was not much display of sanctity. I have a distinct remembrance of one teacher only. He was a yankee, without a family, between 40 and 50 years of age, and wore a matted mass of thick hair over the place where men's ears are usually found. Thus protected, *his* were never seen, and after the opinion spread abroad that by some *misfortune* they had been cut off, he "cut & run."

The infant capital was, still further, the local seat of Justice; and Saturday was for many years, at all times I might say, the regular "term time." Instead of trying cases at home, two or three justices of the peace would come to the "Lick" on that day, and hold their separate courts. This, of course, brought thither all the litigants of the neighbour-hood, with their friends and witnesses. All who wished to purchase at the store would postpone their visit to the same day. All who had to replenish their jugs of whiskey did the same thing. All who had business with others expected to meet them there, as our city merchants, at 12 M. expect to meet each other on "change." Finally, all who thirsted after drink, fun, frolic or fighting, of course, were present. Thus Saturday was a day of largely suspended field labour, but devoted to public business, social pleasure, dissipation, and beastly drunkenness. You might suppose that the presence of civil magistrates would have repressed some of these vices, but it was not so. Each day provided a bill of fare for the next. A new trade in horses, another horse race, a cock fight, or a dog fight, a wrestling match, or a "pitched" battle between two bullies, who in fierce rencontre, would lie on the ground scratching, pulling hair, choking, **goughing** out each others eyes, and biting off each others noses, in the manner of bull dogs, while a Roman circle of interested lookers on would encourage the respective gladiators with shouts which a passing demon might have mistaken for those of hell. In the afternoon the men & boys of business and sobriety would depart, and at nightfall the dissipated would follow them, often two on a horse, reeling and yelling, as I saw drunken Indians do, in the neighbourhood of Fort Leavenworth, in the summer of 1844. But many would be too much intoxicated to mount their horses, and must, therefore, remain till Sunday morning.

I need scarcely tell you that these scenes did not contaminate me. They were quite too gross and wicked to be attractive. On the other hand, they excited disgust, and received from Father the strongest condemnation. I turn from them with pleasure to others of a very different kind.

All the first settlers of Mays Lick were, either by association or profession, Baptists, and had belonged to the church at Scotch Plains, of whom the Revd William Van Horne was the worthy pastor. At what time after their immigration, a house of public worship was erected, I do not remember, but recollect to have attended public worship in Mr. Morris' barn. It happened that most of the Jersey & Virginia families, around the village, were likewise

Baptists, & therefore it was the predominant sect. Hence all my early ideas of Christian doctrine, worship & deportment, were derived from that denomination.

The "Meeting House," as it was always called, was built on a ridge a quarter of a mile south of the village, hard by the great road leading to Lexington. A couple of acres surrounding it constituted the "burying ground" for the station and its neighbourhood.[5] A number of walnut and flowering locust trees had been left standing within the inclosure, and between it, and the "Big road." The house was built of logs, hewn on both sides & had a shingled roof, one of the first I ever saw. The finish of everything was rude and, in winter, it must have been an uncomfortable place. When the weather was warm and dry, however, the rustic edifice, in perfect keeping with the scene around, and with the dress and manners of those who assembled on the sabbath, was attractive, and to this hour constitutes one of my cherished objects of remembrance. No sunday school was taught in it, for none had, at that time, been invented.

Previously to our leaving Mayslick, I had become a regular attendant with father and mother, when not left at home to "mind" the younger children. It was, however, after our removal into the country, that my attendance reached its highest interest. My heart still turns with emotion to the bright and cheerful sabbath mornings, which were to me, like the daily sunshine of an hour, through some opening in the thick leaves of the woods, to

[5] All traces of the "Meeting House" have disappeared but the Mayslick Cemetery is on "the great road" now U.S. Highway No. 68 leading to Lexington.

the little blossoms below. Several things conspired to afford me this delightful effect. It was a day of rest from the labours of the field, and the first thought of the morning included that welcome fact. And yet it was not a morning of idleness, for the stock had to be looked after and disposed of for the day, and there were many household duties to perform before we could leave home. It was, also, a day for dressing up, and none but those who labour through the week, in coarse and dirty clothes, can estimate the cheering influence of a clean face and feet, a clean shirt, and "boughten" clothes on a sabbath morning. All preparation, moreover, had to be finished at an early hour, for to reach the "meeting house" was a work of time. At length, all things ready, and the premises committed to the care of old Lion, we take our departure — mother in a calico dress, with her black silk bonnet covering a newly ironed cap, with the tabs (flaps) tied beneath her chin with a piece of narrow ribbon; father with his shoes just creased and blacked (by myself) with fat & soot, well mixed together; in his shirt sleeves, if the weather were hot, or in his sunday coat, if cool; roram dress-hat over his short, smooth black hair; a bandana handkerchief in his *pocket* for *that* day; and his "walking" stick in his hand, or the baby in his arms; myself in my fustian jacket; with my hat brushed and *set up,* my feet clean, and a new rag on some luckless "stubbed & festering toe"; the younger children in their best sunday clothes; and the whole of us slowly, yet cheerfully — play-fully — moving onward through the cool and quiet woods to the house of God.

The scene around this village temple can never fade from

my memory or my heart. Horses hitched along the fence, and men and women on foot or on horse back, arriving from all quarters; within the inclosure neighbours shaking hands and inquiring after each other's families; a little group leaning against the fence in conversation; another seated on a bench talking "*it over*"; another little party strolling among the graves; and squads of children sitting or lying on the grass to rest themselves.

The hour for worship arrived, the congregation were seated within and around the cabin-church, on benches without backs, and there stood Deacon Morris, a short, broad, grave & fleshy man of 50 beneath the pulpit, giving out the hymn, while Old hundred, by twice as many voices, was mingled with the notes of birds in the surrounding trees.

It was the custom of those who came from a distance to bring with them some kind of food, and in the hour of intermission they might be seen in scattered groups engaged in lunching. Sometimes we returned home to dinner, and did not go again. At other times we dined at Uncle Cornelius Drake's. How impressively all this contrasts with the revolting scenes of Saturday sin and shame which I have described. The village church and the village tavern did in fact represent two great opposing principles: good & evil, — the spirit and the flesh. One might have been taken as the symbol of Heaven — the other of Hell!

P.M. 10 o'c'k. (When I was about to start for Dr Short's[6]

6 Charles Wilkins Short, M. D. (1794-1863), intimate friend and associate of Dr. Drake. He was Professor of Materia Medica and Medical Botany in the Medical Department of the University of Louisville.

where I usually drink tea on Sunday evening, I received a message from Dr **Cartright**[7] of Natchez. So at 7 o'clock, I called on him & brought him to my room, which he has just left.)

It may be interesting to you to know something of the Baptist preachers and the prevalent religious ideas of those days. Most of the former were illiterate persons, but some were men of considerable natural talents. They all lacked dignity & solemnity, and some of them now & then uttered very droll expressions in the pulpit. This was the case with several brothers by the name of Craig, emigrants from Virginia, whose **descendents** are extensively spread over the state of Kentucky.

A great deal of the preaching of those times was doctrinal, I might say, metaphysical, and most of the religious conversation which I heard was of the same kind. Election, reprobation, and predestination were the favourite themes. They were all held strongly *affirmative,* and the slightest doubt was branded as tending to heresy. To these I may add the ordinance of baptism, in reference to which, infant baptism, and sprinkling instead of immersion, were held to be unscriptural. Baptism in the latter mode could not be performed at Mayslick, because there was *not* "much water" there; and as it invariably followed the morning service, long horseback processions were often seen traversing the woods along a narrow road to Lee's creek or Johnson's fork. I sometimes attended them, and certainly nothing could appear more primitive and picturesque than the assembled congregation beneath the green trees on

[7] Samuel A. Cartwright, M. D. (1793-1863).

some sequestered bank. But I refer you to Uncle Benjamin's Tales of the Queen City[8] for the delightful panorama.

Presbyterian ministers occasionally preached in the village; but found little favour with the (predominant) Baptist people. The objections to them, as I well recollect were their advocacy of sprinkling & of infant baptism, and their having been educated in early life to the ministry as to a profession.

The Methodists were, on the main, Marylanders and Virginians — the former predominating. Most of them were among the lamentably ignorant. The high and disorderly excitement which characterized their worship was equally lamentable. Their camp meetings in the woods, which I sometimes attended, presented scenes of fanatical raving among the worshippers, and of levity and vice among the young men who hung about the camp, which were a disgrace to humanity. Their preachers, in point of learning, were even below those of the Baptist connexion. Their dogma of falling from grace, so opposed to the cherished opinions of the latter sect, was that which I oftenest heard in objection to them.

Throughout the whole period of my residence there, I never knew a single Episcopalian. Indeed, I have no recollection of ever hearing the word pronounced. But I heard much of the "Church of England." It was regarded merely

[8] Benjamin Drake (1794-1841), Cincinnati lawyer and author of many interesting sketches of Western scenes in addition to biographies of William Henry Harrison, Black Hawk and Tecumseh. His book to which Dr. Drake refers is *Tales and Sketches from the Queen City* (Cincinnati, 1838) in which there is a description of an outdoor baptism, pages 38-43.

as the persecuting ecclesiastical arm of the British government; an organized body of Arminians, enlisted in the service of despotism. These were Whig ideas of the Revolutionary war, so lately passed through, and were not very far from being true: — as you may convince yourself by reading the lives of **Westley,** Venn & Simeon, which show us the condition of the English Church about the middle of the last century. The persecutors of John Rogers[9] and John Bunyan were not likely to be regarded with much favour by those who had learned their letters in a primer, which in one of its rude cuts presented the former at the stake surrounded by his wife and nine children; and who afterwards read the Pilgrim's progress more than any other book, except the bible. It is somewhat remarkable that, thoroughly imbued as I was in boyhood with these traditional opinions, prejudices and feelings, the first Episcopal Church of Cincinnati should afterwards have been organized in my house, and that I should have subsequently attached myself to that Communion. My predilection for Baptist worship was, however, of a decided character, and if that Church had possessed a written creed, a system of Church government beyond the democracy of the Congre-

[9] Dr. Drake is mistaken. The cause for the persecution of John Rogers was entirely different from that of John Bunyan. Concerning the former, see Footnote No. 10 Letter VII. An ardent Catholic, Queen Mary I was responsible for the death of John Rogers. John Bunyan (1628-1688) merely incurred the displeasure of the Church of England for preaching too openly and vehemently without a license. For this, in 1666, he was thrown into prison where he remained until 1672. During this time he was apparently allowed many liberties. After his release he began preaching again and encountered little interference.

gation, and an educated Clergy, I presume I should have
continued within its borders.

I must now pass on to some details which will bring me
back to the fireside and the field, but will first make an
application to myself of what I have said on the history of
a Community which is now nearly extinct.

1ˢᵗ You must have perceived that I was educated, till 15
years of age, in a state of society which presented the
opposing elements of virtue & vice, piety and profanity, in
many of their most lovely and hideous forms. Thus I came,
at an early period, to understand both, and to admire the
one while I detested the other. If I had not seen the wicked-
ness, the righteousness displayed around me would have
appeared less beautiful: if I had seen *it* only, I might,
notwithstanding its manifold deformities, have been drawn
into a participation more extensive than I was.

2ᵈ As our community was made up of recent immigrants
from different states, my mind was enlarged by association
with them: my knowledge of character extended. As they
were from slave holding and a non slave holding state
(for Jersey was practically such) I saw the two varieties of
character which our country presents. I had them before
me, in *juxta position*, every day, and could & did compare
their opinions, prejudices, feelings, manners, customs, and
modes of life. These were important opportunities for a
boy—real, substantial food for a young mind—and served,
in the absence of schools and book studies, to promote its
growth. Thus my early advantages were not so limited after

all, as I have sometimes, in seeking excuses for not having risen higher in the world, endeavoured to persuade myself. (As it is now past 12 o'c'k & I wish to write to brother Charles, I must bid you—*Good night.*)

Monday 11 P.M. You will think, my Echo, this rather a late and drowsy hour to return to my elongated epistle, which in your mother tongue signifies—long letter. Nevertheless, there is no harm in my return, it is only the stupid things I may write, that you ought to regret. As they are likely to be very miscellaneous, I know not which to take up first, but dull as I am, I have sense enough to perceive that *being* miscellaneous, it is of no importance with which I begin. I shall, therefore, enter on one which happens (by the way) to be pretty closely connected with the latter part of what I wrote yesterday.

It was not only my favoured destiny to have pious parents, but a pious Uncle & Aunt—in Uncle Cornelius & Aunt Lydia Drake, both of whom were staid & sober minded theologians—more deeply read in the Bible & theological works than Father & mother. Aunt had rather a masculine cast of mind, and Uncle would, with proper education, have made a good *judge.* They were much at our house, and we were much at theirs, and I heard a great deal of religious, or at least, theological conversation between them and my parents. I received from them much good advice and admonition, which greatly strengthened the impression made by the advice I received at home. And this leads me to believe, that friends and relatives might often aid each other in the discipline & moral government of their children. What is said to us (while young) by others than our parents has an aspect of disinterestedness, and is regarded. The same thing said by a father or mother might seem to us merely a matter of present discipline; and may go but a little way towards forming our principles. The advice of Uncle, when I was about to leave home for C., where he thought I would encounter many new temptations, was more judicious and effective than that of Father.

I must again advert to the polemic Divinity of the Baptists, by whom I was surrounded. At a very early period, long before I left home, their conversation and debates with others had given a cast of that kind to my own mind. Such questions as to the origin of sin, the universality of redemption, and the nature of future punishment had begun to receive attention. Not that I doubted the Bible, for my traditional faith was perfect, I only sought to understand things which seemed obscure—which I *now* perceive are obscure because they are *transcendental*. At that time I had not drawn the distinction between the attainable and the transcendental.

Throughout the period of which I am writing, my thoughts were strongly turned on a future state. Heaven filled my imagination by day, and I was ever seeking to form a conception of it. By night, in sleep, the idea did not leave me, and I dreamt, times without number, of witnessing the day of Judgement, and of being in Heaven.

It was a kind of popular credulity, at that time, that the world would come to an end at the close of the 18th century, and as it was near that period, I lived in expectation of it. I remember, when 10 or 11 years old, to have got hold of a little piece, written as I *understood* by Dr. Franklin, who knew a great deal, that spoke of human beings as being like Ephemera which lived only *18* hours. Such was my monomania on this subject, that it seemed to me an additional evidence, that at the end of 1800 years, from the birth of the Saviour, the end of the world would happen. So great was my dread on this point, that any uncommon appearance in the heavens always suggested that the time had arrived. About the age I have just mentioned, when I was hoeing corn in the field one afternoon by myself, there formed in the east a great thunder cloud (a very rare phenomenon), and the lightnings were playing in it, with distant thunder, for a couple of hours. Terror and awe of the most solemn kind were inspired in me. Although I did not, like many of the Millerites of modern days, abandon my work, the impression made upon me was so strong, that down to the present time I can yet recall the aspect of the cloud. The change which has taken place in my *feelings* is so great, that I should meet the end of *all* things with more composure than a solitary death. Such, at least, is my opinion. Since the grand and terrible idea of the last day, which filled the imagination of my childhood, has been moulded into its present form, I no longer dream of it; & I certainly cannot regret, that it then existed. I believe that it not only preserved me from some of the vices of that time of life, but contributed to elevate my conceptions and increase my poetical temperament. The feelings I then had, if not the expectation, ought, in my opinion, to be cherished. Our sensibilities to things

spiritual & heavenly too often become blunted by the influence of the cares and duties and interests of life; so large
a portion of which are sensual and groveling, that all the
"thoughts & imaginations of our hearts" become gross and
limited. To have dignity, elevation, purity, and expansion,
they must range into the infinite and borrow something
from the mysterious. When every child in the world shall
be found a firm and faithful believer, in what I so implicitly
believed, the human race will be in a much better condition than at present: always provided, however, that moral
precepts, and not an interceding & sacrificing priesthood,
be engrafted on the belief. It is the latter & that only, which
renders the kind of superstition which I have described
injurious to mankind. But as it's near 1 o'c'k A.M. I am
quite too drowsy to pursue a subject of such magnitude &,
therefore, — *Adieu.*

Tuesday 2 P.M. (I find that when I broke off last night,
I was not so drowsy as I fancied, for I did not sleep well,
was in fact poorly about the head, & had been for 12 hours.
I have continued so till now; having had some difficulty in
expressing my disjointed and reluctant thoughts at my
lecture this forenoon.)

What is called a superstitious belief is the greatest of
all moral power, or among the greatest and, *in itself*, neither
good nor bad. A mere force, but a force which has its main-
spring in *some* unvisited—unseen & mysterious region. It
is the knowledge, true or false, which the individual has
or believes he has, concerning that region, which deter-
mines the character and effects of his superstition. The

Indian dies calmly, because he believes that he will immediately join the companions who have gone before him, in delightful hunting grounds, at the further end of death's path—the milky way. The Philippic Greeks died with composure for they believed that the gods always rewarded virtue. One wicked man, in a Christian Country, dies in agony of soul, because he expects everlasting punishment. Another dies in stolid **indiference,** because his superstition has been "rooted out." The doubting Christian dies, in apprehension, *because* he doubts. The Christian whose faith is strong and firm dies in corresponding hope and peace, for he expects to join the blessed company of the redeemed & has no pangs but those which are connected with the sundering of his earthly affections.

In all cases, other things being equal, the **tranquilly** or the dismay, will be according to the strength of the belief: of the superstition as it might, philosophically, be called. What, then? Are these different Systems to be placed on one level? By no means. They agree only in the principle of belief—they disagree in its objects.

Christ did not come into the world to implant in us new principles, but was "a teacher sent from God!" He came to instruct us concerning Heaven and Hell, and to tell us how to escape the latter & reach the former. He came to turn our superstition on Himself & command us how to live, and those commandments embrace all our moral & religious duties. When instructed in these we become upright and holy in life, in proportion to our superstition, that is our faith—the knowledge of things unseen, but believed to exist, because he has declared it.

Now if all children were thus taught, and their *natural* belief in the *super* natural were cherished instead of being repressed, would they not be brought into the ways of holiness, from the broad beaten roads of sin, by a more powerful influence than any other known to the human will? Most certainly. And no inefficiency, no weakness of character, in reference to the proper duties & pursuits of human life would be the result, but the very reverse. In proportion as they continued to believe the command to practice virtue and abhor vice, to be from God, they would be bold and active in its observance. The superstition would constitute the strength of their character till death.

Having stumbled inadvertently into this disquisition, I must add a few pages before I leave it.

1. When a system of sacrificial observances is substituted for the Commandments of God—there is no lack of faith, but the duties which the individual is taught to perform are different from those taught & enjoined by the saviour. Instead of being strengthened in character, he is weakened; as you may assure yourself by comparing the people who live under that system with those who live under the system of Christ: as the people of Italy with those of Prussia, the people of Spain with those of England, and the people of Mexico with those in the United States.

2. The pernicious influence of any & every departure from the system of Christ, and the effects of following it, in all its simplicity—the utter degradation of character in one case, and its purity, dignity and elevation in the other, is, and ever must be to all sound & reflecting minds, one

of the strongest arguments in favour of its Divine origin.[10]

My superstition, and that of the people of Mayslick, in the days of which I am writing, extended to other things than Heaven & Hell. It embraced omens, ghosts, and even the self motion of dead men's bones. Some cabins were startled by strange sounds. A night or two before the death of my cousin Dr. John Drake, some member of the family heard the sound of a plane, as in preparing boards for a coffin. The barking of dogs during the severe illness of a person was ominous of death. The arm or thigh bone of a man who had been buried on a spot which was afterwards cultivated, was exhumed, I do not remember how or why, but it was reburied, and afterwards appeared on the surface of the ground! For myself, if not a firm believer in these specimens of the supernatural, they were so established in my imagination, that I was always, when alone in the dark, in a kind of expectation or fear that something would show itself from the world of mystery. That apprehension is gone; but darkness and solitude, in certain situations, by an association of ideas, still bring up images of that kind. Such displays of belief in the invisible world are the offspring of ignorance or bad education, & should be got rid of, not by attacking and diminishing our principle of superstition, but turning it on proper objects by the right kind of instruction.

(*P.M. 9 o'c'k.* I have just returned from the Hall of the University, where Dr. Cartwright, of Natchez delivered

[10] The seven paragraphs immediately preceding were omitted from the previous edition of this book.

a second lecture. The first was delivered last night, both at the request of the class, and both so well received that the publication of them has been asked & the copy granted. They were on statistical medicine & empyricism.)[11]

We had at the period of which I write several common and current credulities, which were not superstitions, though they are erroneously called so. Nothing is a superstition which does not look to a spiritual world; but the opinions & practices to which I now refer, were limited to matter. They went beyond our earth, but not beyond the material universe. A belief in the influence of the moon not only on the atmosphere, but on vegetation and even animal life, was common. Thus, radishes must be planted at the decrease of the moon, for they tapered downwards & so of some other vegetables. Others still, must be planted or sowed in the increase of that orb. And hogs must not be killed in the dark or decrease of that luminary, for the pork would shrink and waste away in the barrel. Then there were the "12 signs of the Zodiac" presiding over the 12 different parts of the living body in the 12 months of the year. These parts were indicated in an abominable frontispiece, surrounded by the symbolic signs & names of the 12 constellations of the Zodiac; but where or what the Zodiac was, no one knew. Old M[r] Guthrie, the grammarian

---

[11] The first lecture of Dr. Cartwright, *Statistical Medicine or Numerical Analysis Applied to the Investigation of Morbid Conditions* was published in *The Western Journal of Medicine and Surgery,* Vol. I (New Series): 185-206, March 1848, of which Dr. Drake was one of the Editors. Apparently the second lecture was never published.

of Geography, at length gave me some insight into this remnant of Astrology. Notwithstanding our ignorance, or rather, in consequence of it, we believed that many things must be done, or left undone, during the reign of each constellation. Therefore, the almanac was an important book of reference. It would not be safe even to wean a baby without consulting the oracle!

Having mentioned this greatest of all periodicals, as to the extent of its circulation, I am led to remark that it was, after the necessary tables, composed of the most abominable trash that could be collected—anecdotes, *bon mots*, Jokes & short stories, often profane and still oftener, licentious. The only exception was "Poor Richard's Almanac," which presented a mass of *worldly* wisdom most admirable in its way. As our almanacs were all imported from Philadelphia, they must have been specimens of the best published in the United States at that time—say half a century ago. At the present day there are humorous Almanacs published, but there are others abounding in valuable matter on rural and domestic economy; others more especially fitted for cities; others suited to the taste and interests of political parties; others adapted to different religious denominations; and all, except the first, are on the side of morality, or morality and religion. Two great facts are indicated by this change of character. 1st A division, or rather something corresponding to a division, of labour; 2^{d} An improved taste in morals & religion. The former shews a vast increase of population—the latter, a delightful increase in refinement & piety:—Important revolutions in the state of society, to occur in *part* of the lifetime of one individual.

Whenever I am writing of our ignorance, the Maryland element of our population comes into my mind. Several of Father's nearest neighbours, one of his tenants (for small as was his little tract of land, only 200 acres, he had three), were immigrants from that state. They were not only extremely ignorant compared with the Jersey, and *most* of the Virginia immigrants, in all school learning, but likewise in the domestic arts. I was told that one family had purchased half a pound of Bohea tea, and boiled it in winter with a ham of bacon in place of greens! I myself remember to have seen in a family to which Father sent me on an errand, early in the morning, a quantity of tea boiling in a large uncovered "Dutch oven" (as it was then called), out of which they were dipping it with a tin cup and drinking it from the breakfast table. Many of them were indolent, and more than an equal number "given to drink." The religious portion were chiefly Methodists, a fact which I have already mentioned.

My father's Maryland tenant was named Hickman. The first lodgment of his family was in a tree top in the month of May, the tree with a heavy garniture of green leaves being cut down for that purpose. But father had already built a small stable without a floor, which was not wanted at that season of the year, and, as soon as it could be cleaned out they removed into it, cooking by a fire on the outside, till a cabin was built near to father's. This man had a wife older and proportionably larger than himself, with two or three little children. He was very poor, and yet owned a negro man in middle life, and a woman rather old—at least twice the age of himself. His treatment of both was cruel in the extreme. A single pair of the flimsiest (negro) shoes was all the man got in the year, and the old woman was quite as miserably clothed. They were fed on stinted diet. Both worked in the field, and were pushed under the whip to the extremest degree. Its use on the man did not excite our feelings so much as that on the old woman. She had been his nurse in infancy, and yet he would tie her up, strip her back naked, and whip her with a cowhide till the blood would flow to her feet, and her screams would reach our ears at the distance of more than 300 yards. Of course, we were greatly delighted when he left us. All the masters of the neighbourhood were not as cruel as this man; but the treatment generally of negroes at that time was severe, as to food, clothing, punishment, and required service, compared with what it now is, even far in the south, and of course was *barbarous* compared with the present regimen over Kentucky generally; another evidence of the amelioration of society.

Of all the Jersey immigrants father, I think, was the only one who did not become a slave holder. Even good old Uncle Cornelius purchased a man by the name of Clem, and argued from the Bible that it was right. Whether right or wrong, Clem had great cause to rejoice, for he was treated kindly, never perhaps received a blow, was incorporated into the family, and lived to old age. He also purchased a woman. In 1800 his only son, Jacob, married the daughter of Judge Conway, a Virginian, who had negroes, and Jacob also purchased one or two. Eighteen years afterwards *I* purchased from him two negro children, a brother & sister, Carlos & Hannah, 11 and 9 years of age, and brought them to Cincinnati, by which they were emancipated, & had them bound to me by the overseers of the poor, till they should become of age. Hannah was of course your nurse.

One of our Jersey neighbours, "Old Billy Dye," as he was always called, a pushing kind of farmer, also purchased negroes. I was often sent to his house on errands, and one day I reached his door just in time to hear the last blows and groans of a whipping. The slave came out in agony & tears, & the floor was strewn with fragments of the rod, over which he stood in the rage of a demon. On returning home, I related the whole to father, whose blood welled with indignation, and he demanded to know if I did not speak out and let the old man have my mind; becoming almost angry with me because I had "held my peace." This man had daughters, who brought disgrace on his name, and his two sons, after marrying, died confirmed drunkards. Still his was one of my principal visiting houses, and one of the most *fashionable* places of resort for the young people of the neighbourhood.

The first Constitution of Kentucky was adopted in 1791 [actually April 19, 1792], three years after we entered the State; the second, 8 years afterwards [1799]. Pending *its* adoption, a very strong effort was made over the state to elect members of the Convention who would favour the *gradual* abolition of Slavery. Mr Clay,[12] who had just arrived at Lexington, united himself with that party, and laboured in the good cause. I need scarcely tell you that

[12] Henry Clay (1777-1852), friend and admirer of Dr. Drake from their first meeting to the death of Clay.

your grandfather was of the same party. In fact, he was one of its most impassioned members; and all my own thoughts and feelings took the same direction. The discussions, public & private, were numerous, and the excitement ran so high that Phil. Thomas, a politician of some note, declared that he would wade to his knees in blood before it should take place. He lately died at Baton Rouge, La., in his 80th year, under the title of General Philemon Thomas.

For several years before I left home, father with some of his neighbours talked a great deal about moving off to Ohio—then called The Territory, and actually made a visit of exploration into the valley of Paint Creek & Chillicothe, then a new village, extending it thence to the Miami Country. They returned loud in their praises of the Paint Creek bottoms (on which you and I have so often taken drives), and also of the L. Miami valley. Why they did not remove, I can not tell; but I remember the motives for removal, which led them to meditate it: 1st The existence of slavery in Kentucky; 2^{d} The uncertainty of land titles; 3^{d} The want of good water. Had he removed at that time, when I was about 13 years of age, the necessity & value of my services in opening a new farm would have no doubt prevented my studying medicine. I might now have been a farmer, supplying families in Cincinnati with good *clean* butter, and acting at home as a justice of the peace, a school trustee, or an overseer of the poor! To all of which duties, I should have been better adapted, than to my present high responsibilities. (As it is 12 o'c'k again, *Bonne Nuit.*)

Wednesday ½ past 9 A.M. (D[r] Cartwright is to call on me at 10, to go to the Library[13] & Museum of our University & spend the forenoon in them, while I am preparing for & delivering my lecture from 11 to 12—So while waiting for him, I take up my reminiscential pen, to lay it down when he may enter.)

I register the slavery discussion, of which I have given you some notice, among my early advantages, not only giving me information, but exciting thought. I may refer to some others of a kindred character.

The outbreak of the French Revolution occurred when I was about 4 or 5 years old, and excited a deep emotion over the U.S. The aid which France had rendered us in our Revolutionary Struggle was still fresh in the memory of the people, and their hearts were of course in sympathy with the French, whom great masses of our citizens would have willingly assisted by going to war with England. Gen[l] Washington opposed himself to this policy. Jn[o] Adams succeeded him; and both were regarded by the zealous & grateful well wishers to struggling France, as leaning to England, from which the sword had so lately severed us. To raise money for the support of our government, as we had but little commerce to afford impost duties, certain direct taxes were levied by M[r] Adams' administration, among which was an excise duty on distilleries and their products. Also, I believe, a "stamp-act" or duty on paper to be used for deeds, notes & other documents, all of which

[13] The medical library of the University of Louisville contained 3,216 volumes, and of the medical libraries in the United States at this time was probably surpassed only by that of Transylvania University.

had been among those measures of the British Government which led us to rebel. These acts of Mr Adams' administration were attacked with violence and virulence by the Republican press, as it was then called; and to defend itself from these assaults, that administration had the weakness to enact a Sedition law. Such was the highly exciting state of national politics, from my 10th to my 15th year inclusive. No part of the Union experienced the excitement in a higher degree than Old Mason,[14] except perhaps Sister Belle's (Western Pennsylvania) where an actual insurrection was embodied (in which, to some extent, if I am not mistaken) both her father and Albert Gallatin (for whom your grandfather called a son, born soon afterwards) took a hand. Now, as from my earliest recollection of public affairs, I had a great deal of feeling and sympathy with them, I could not fail to be an attentive listener, and, of course, an apt scholar, throughout the period which has been designated. In looking back upon it, I am persuaded that the school was a real source of intellectual improvement.

Mr Jefferson became the Candidate of the party to which I, at the age of 12, belonged. On the 4th of March, 1801, when he was inaugurated as President of the United States, 3 months after I commenced the study of medicine, I wrote, and sitting alone in my chamber in a small white farm house, where Mrs Genl Lytle now resides, drank, in cold water, thirteen toasts in celebration of the triumphant event! This little piece of veritable history shows that the workings of our popular institutions are in fact efficient

14 Mason County, Kentucky.

causes of intellectual growth in our boys. [It] explains why we have so many able statesmen, lawyers, and divines, who have never been submitted to the teachings of the University.

(Dr. Cartwright has arrived and I must start to our own University, to leave him among its books & dry bones, while I lecture to the students on *Asiatic* Cholera: so, once more farewell!)

2 P.M. In a despotic country, such a country boy as I was, could never have heard any of the discussions in religion and politics to which I had so many opportunities of listening. Nor could he have had any lively sensibility to those or other great interests, which, like a healthy appetite to the body, favour the development of mind. I had not only variety of character, but variety of topics, presented to me. While none of the former were intellectually high—many of the latter were of great magnitude, and the very apprehension of them served to enlarge the horizon of my childhood; while the diversities of character greatly augmented the area of my social sympathies, especially in the humbler walks of life.

Had I a retentive memory for details, and a power of delineation, I could draw you a number of portraits that would display many original features. I know too well my incapacity to venture on any thing of the kind, but may refer in a few paragraphs to two or three of them.

"Old Billy Johnson" mentioned in a former letter, lived a mile or more west of Father's, and was one of the owners of the "Pond," where he had a small tanyard. He was also a cobbler and a farmer. He had 2 or 3 daughters and 5 sons, all older than myself. His good old, equable, motherly and pious wife, Charity, was my father's cousin. He was a man of some reading, but distinguished for his oddities and his sudden flashings of impatience or petty anger. He was a great talker, had a historical memory, had lived in Jersey and Virginia before he came to Kentucky, and I learned (imperfectly) many things from him. His young son, Abram, a little older than myself—he always called Aby my pigeene! Among the anecdotes told of him I recollect but two distinctly. He and his sons would frequently breakfast in common on mush and milk out of a huge buckeye bowl, each one dipping in his spoon. When the old gentleman happened to be in a hurry and wished to have them all in the field as quick as possible, he would eat in the manner of the rest, till they came towards the bottom, then throw down his spoon, pick up the bowl with both hands, drink off the remainder, jump up, and saying they had all "eat enough," start away.

Once when he and good old aunt Charity were sitting in Darby & Joan style by the door of the cabin, he was fixing in the clapper of a cow bell, rather a perplexing affair at best, & the flash of petulance took the direction of his right arm, and, as was his custom, shutting his eyes he slung the "tarnal thing" into the flax patch in front of the house. In a minute the paroxysm was over, and he inquired in the mildest tones:—*"Honey, did you see where the bell lit?"* Charity had noticed the spot and the offender was reclaimed and restored to favour. How often, under the influence of our passions, we do things which require us to appeal to charity!

"Old Rector" was another original of those days. He was born and "raised" in the Valley of Virginia, in the neighbourhood of Winchester or "Rumny" as he was wont to call the town of Romney. Afterwards he lived a long time on Chartier's Creek, or the "Shirtee," as he pronounced it, South of Pittsburg in Western Pennsylvania, when it was almost a wilderness. Thence he removed & settled (for a time) as a kind of squatter, by the best spring of the neighbourhood, about half a mile from Father's. He went there one or two years before us. It was from his spring that I and the boys of the neighbourhood used to "tote" drinking and cooking water, in a "dry time." The scene in the morning was not unlike that presented at some of the wells of Judea, 1800 years before, for many of the visitors were women. This old man had a wife who was infirm and scarcely ever left the house—a couple of daughters, one of whom was nearly idiotic—two grown sons, the younger of whom was a fat (going at large) fool; the older a great simpleton, with an upper jaw shaped like that of a snapping turtle, and projecting over the lower further than I have ever seen either before or since. Not one of the family, from the father to the youngest child, could either read or write. There were other children, married and living off at a greater distance. Such, for the first two years, were our nearest neighbours. The names of the boys were John & Dan, and I was with them a great deal, when 9, 10 & 11 years of age. Such is the sympathy of mind between children and adults of feeble intellect. Happily they had no gross vices, and being good tempered we got on without injury to either party. But I must return to the old man. He had nearly all his life been a great hunter—was in fact a large coarse Leather Stocking—and still depended much on his rifle for the means of subsistence, as he cultivated but little land. For several years he was our most frequent visitor, especially from the time that white frosts set in till the nights got short at the close of the ensuing spring. He generally came after supper, and would mostly sit till father would go out, leave the door open & talk to him about the height and appearance of the moon, the stars or the clouds. He was a large, raw boned, good natured, homely, grotesque, talkative old man, and had a never ending vein of disjointed narrative of the past, as he had seen it about "Rumny" & on the "Shirtee," and "round Pitt." How much my own historical and auto-biographical reminiscences are modeled after him! Father and mother often got tired of his visits, as they were not more protracted than his conversation was repetitious; but to me they were otherwise, and I hailed his coming.

What he said about the Valley of Virginia indicated that it had, at the middle of the last Century, rather a rude, vulgar, and turbulent population. His stories of the "Shirtee" and "Pitt" made on my memory a deeper impression. He was familiar with the names and family circumstances of Gen¹ Morgan & his son or, brother in law, Gen¹ Neville. I believe that between his wife and one of those families there was some relationship. His character and condition were so low that I never ventured to inquire of Morgan Neville[15] concerning it.

He was an implicit believer in witchcraft, and "raising" & "laying" the Devil. Concerning the last, he related that when he lived on the "Shirtee," he had seen a preacher with the Bible in his hand "lay" the Devil under one of the posts of a fence; which I thought a very remarkable feat. His residence, in that region, had given him an exhaustless fund of *material* on the Indians, Indian wars & Indian fighters. He was familiar (in his way) with the life and exploits of Simon Kenton—knew Cresap personally & all about the murder of the family of Logan, the Mingo Chief. He often excited my imagination & feelings by his account of the burning on the Sandusky of Colonel Crawford[16] by the Delawares, in 1782. Sixty years after that tragedy, and 48 years after its first Citation to me, when I was on the banks of the Tyamochtee, a branch of the Sandusky, I was searching for some remaining black coal of the fire which once shone so flamingly in my "mind's eye," the image of my first teacher in Western history (the simple hearted, illiterate, garrulous old man) was constantly before me, but could not point out the exact spot where Crawford was burnt. It was, however, hard by the Rail road track, and as the cars roll along, the ashes of the Martyr rise in the air, and are

[15] Morgan Neville (1786-1839), son of Gen. Presley Neville (1756-1818), and grandson of Gen. Daniel Morgan, both of whom distinguished themselves during the Revolution. Morgan Neville, editor, author, musician and patron of art, was an intimate friend of Dr. Drake in Cincinnati.

[16] Colonel William Crawford (1732-1782), Revolutionary soldier, surveyor and friend of Washington. He led an unsuccessful expedition against the Indians, was captured, tortured and finally burned at the stake.

unconsciously breathed by thousands of *ladies* & *gentle-men,* who have never even pronounced his name, for they never read the history of their own country.

But the cherished theme of the old man was hunting and trapping. With the methods of taking wolves by building a small cabin and placing in it a piece of meat, attached to something which kept open the door, that would shut and latch itself when the meat was seized; and with the mode of "setting" and "baiting" a trap, I became as familiar as other boys elsewhere were at the same time with the declension of Latin adjectives. From him I first learned, that when his foreleg is caught in the "steel trap," the wolf will sometimes gnaw off his foot, and escape. That seemed to me very remarkable, for I did not know, or think, that the pressure would benumb the parts below the teeth of the trap. The old man garrulous, also taught me the sounds imitative of the wild turkey's "gobble," by which that silly and unsuspecting bird, at the dawn of day, might be drawn near the log behind which the hunter was concealed. Then he would impress the teaching with stories of one hunter killing another who was imitating the gobble of a turkey.

Deer hunting, however, seemed to have been Old Leather Stocking's cherished pursuit. Its results were clothing, food, & fiddle strings for the Banjo. In the preceptive part of his Nimrodic occupation I became quite *au fait.* The best seasons of the year were made familiar to me: then you must not hunt, after the leaves have fallen, when the weather is dry, but wet, for the animal will hear you at a great distance; nor in windy weather, as he will smell you equally as far, unless you have the sagacity to get on the right side of him before you know where he is; nor when a snow is falling, for you can not track him, nor follow him by his blood if you have wounded him; but may do both with great success after the "snow holds up." I was not less familiar with the "ambush" (ambuscade) of the deer-lick. You must go in the night and construct it, at a suitable distance, of green bushes, conceal yourself in it, and watch till the dawn of day when the animal comes to drink, and then "draw a sight" upon his head, or behind his fore shoulders. Finally, the old man often detailed the processes for "dressing" buckskins, in which both he and myself were generally in part clothed. Thus it was that in many series of winter nights, I learned many things of no particular value in themselves, but they were suggestive, excited curiosity, and kept my mind in a state of activity. I therefore regard them as having been useful to me, and class the old hunter among my school masters.

Mr Rector, as I ought to call him after acknowledging him as one of my teachers, had a married daughter whose husband's name was "Billy Rhodes." He lived near to Aunt Lydia Tennant, two miles from our house, and having children near my own age, I was often there. He also had a father who resided with him; but for whom I should not mention the family. Old Mr Rhodes, or "Grand-daddy" as the children called him, was a man of large frame, very meanly dressed, with a rude and extensive white beard. When I most frequently saw him, he must have been, as it now appears to me, nearly 90 years of age. He staid constantly in the little cabin, & much of the time in bed. He was silent, childish, & morose, seemed to have no sympathy with those around him, and they appeared to have but little care or affection for him, who was their terror. His aspect, and the relations of the family with him, made on my feelings and memory an ineffaceable impression. I had never before, nor scarcely since, seen the forlorn and repulsive character of extreme old age so impressively illustrated. I believe that to the sad spectacle which he exhibited to me 53 or 4 years ago, I may trace up much of my dread of falling, at that advanced period of life, out of communion of mind and heart with children, grand children, and great grand children. When an old man is found in this desolate isolation — those around him praying that he would die, instead of labouring to make him comfortable & cheerful — the fault is generally, I presume, in himself; for it is more reasonable to believe one person to be wrong in feeling & conduct, than a whole family.

Mr Rector had a married son, living in the same neighbourhood with Rhodes whose name was Charles. I introduce him here because he exerted, strange to say, at least a *nominal* influence on your brother! Being the most respectable member of the old gentleman's family, he was often the topic of conversation, and always designated by his father under the endearing appellation of — Charly. As I did not relish what related to Charly as much as what was told of Logan, Cresap, and Crawford, I became at last utterly tired and disgusted with the name. Sixteen or seventeen years afterwards, while I was engaged in the study of Botany, with the *Systema Naturae* of Carolus Linnaeus for my guide, I had become so enamoured with the character of the great swedish Naturalist, that I determined to call my first born son after him; but having my old aversion to Charly, I charged everybody to call him Charles! As he was not baptized, I kept his middle name in the background, intending to give it or not according to his future taste for natural history, or his promise of distinction in letters & science. He was told, however, that a middle name was in reserve for him, if he should prove worthy of it. I waited till he was about fifteen, and then, had to substitute my own, for that of the Naturalist of the north—had I waited longer, I should not have done it.[17]

Speaking of a neighbour of my aunt **Tennant** reminds me of her death, and of the sorrow into which it threw us, for she was an amiable sister and aunt, and our visitings were delightful. The loss to mother was especially severe. Immediately after the birth of her second daughter, she was taken ill with what I now know, from what was said, to have been puerperal fever. Mother was with her, and father went there one morning, and returned, telling us that he must go to "town" (Washington) for Dr Goforth. I well remember seeing him trot off in his clean shirt sleeves with the dirt rubbed off his shoes, and his Sunday hat on his head. The D^r was in the country, and they did not get out until in the night. We had to stay alone. The next day father and mother came back, and told us that Aunt Lydia was dead! It was the first death, except of young children, that had occurred among us, and we were very sorrowful. To console us, father

---

[17] Charles D. Drake at this time was headstrong, and had run away from school. His father was deeply disappointed in him. Dr. Drake then gave him his own name instead of that of Linnaeus. Later Charles Daniel settled down and became a successful lawyer.

took out of his pocket some rolls of cinnamon bark, which Cousin John Drake, then a student of medicine, had given him. It was the first I had ever tasted, and the impression made by it on the body was so associated with the emotion of mind, that from that time to this, I have scarcely ever seen a roll of Cinnamon bark, without thinking of the early fate of my good Aunt Lydia.

A year or so after this melancholy event, another occurred of an opposite kind, but again especially affecting Mother. I was "minding the cow" at the cabin door, where she was eating slop early one morning, while mother milked her. In the midst of it, a stranger on foot walked slowly up and spoke to me. Mother heard him—looked round—rose to her feet—stood "stock still," and burst into tears, with loud convulsive sobbing. I was perfectly astounded, but in a moment they were clasped in each other's arms—it was her oldest brother, Manning Shotwell, who she had not seen for eight years. I suppose that as many letters had scarcely passed between them. He was a poor man, & having lost his wife had determined to visit us. He walked from Jersey to Fort Pitt, and then took water to Limestone, whence he walked out to Mayslick, which he reached late in the evening & so remained all night at Uncle's. Father was out on the farm; and at length returning, our good old black walnut breakfast table rejoiced in having round it the happiest family in all "Kentuck!" Uncle remained with us for several weeks; and as the conversation embraced an account of everything he could say about Jersey and our relations there, & all that father & mother could tell him of our Journey out, and our lives to that time, it was quite an occasion of mental improvement to myself—always an interested and attentive listener. *Good Evening.*

P.M. 11 o'c'k I broke off at 8, to visit Dr Gross,[18] who had invited 15 or 20 physicians to meet Dr Cartwright. I wore my new clothes. How amazingly cheering it is to be dressed up now and then! The *philosophy* of *dressing* is not much better understood than many other philosophies. To understand it well, a man must have been a poor boy, and known the happiness conferred by an occasional new wool hat, or new pair of brass "slee' buttons"—price ninepence; and having known this, possess the means and time to dress up occasionally in after life.[19] He who is always highly dressed, not less than the sloven who never dresses, knows little of the enjoyment which comes from being now and then (periodically as it were) rigged out in a genteel, first rate, quality suit, such as I now sit writing in,—for I concluded to keep it on after I came back, as it was 11 o'c'k. However, I took off my coat and put on my autumnal *Robe de Chambre,* as I might possibly get an ink spot on it.

It appeared to me that I was better dressed than any other gentleman in the room and I had a good opportunity for judging. While they were busy, talking with each other, I now and then took a walk up and down the long drawing

[18] Samuel David Gross, M. D. (1805-1884), close friend, admirer and associate of Dr. Drake in Cincinnati and in Louisville. Dr. Gross was Professor of Surgery in the Medical Department of the University of Louisville.

[19] The remainder of this and all of the following paragraph did not appear in the edition of this book edited by Charles D. Drake.

room, in a natural kind of way, as if I were thinking of something important, so that they should not surmise my object. While doing so, I carelessly glanced at the great opposite mirrors and was thus able to compare my image with that of each of the members of the party. Being a little (I hope not unjustifiably) elated by this comparison, I withdrew to the dining room where I knew I should find M[rs] Gross and her sister M[rs] Casey, who looked at me with an expression which a gentleman is fond of seeing in ladies, when he thinks he has on a nice kind of dress.[20] After sipping a cup of coffee with them, I started home, to resume my letter, which I now proceed to do.

Not long after Uncle Manning left us, we had another visitor from Jersey, whose arrival excited a more general interest. He was no other man than the Rev. William Van Horne,[21] the old Scotch Plains' pastor of the five families who had emigrated in 1788, and has been already mentioned. No other man living could have produced so deep an impression on the hearts of the whole. Several of them had been communicants in his church, and all belonged to his congregation. Like the rest he had been a staunch Whig, and during the Revolution acted as Chaplain. He still wore a three cornered cocked hat, dressed in black broad cloth, was a fine looking old gentleman, of good intelligence, and now and then fell into a fit of laughter that would make his

[20] Dr. Drake's elation in this instance should be compared with the contrasting embarrassment which he describes in Letter V, page 106.

[21] Rev. William Van Horne (?-1807), pastor of the Scotch Plains (New Jersey) Baptist Church from December 15, 1785 to October 4, 1807.

face as red as if it had been tinted with Carmine. Of course, all the sources of hospitality which the five families could draw upon, were pumped dry. Father and mother's turn at length came. He and several of our Mayslick relations were to spend the day, & dine with us. Whatever could be done the day before in the way of putting things "to rights," was of course performed, and the next morning we were up "bright and early." Lizy and I were (willingly) taxed to the extent of our skill. The best sweet potato hills were opened; the washing of the long yellow potatoes, among other things, devolved on me. I recollect that when mother laid them in a dutch oven and poured a little water on them, they looked beautiful. Altogether the day passed off "very fine," and afforded us new topics of conversation for a long time.

Parson Van Horne preached for us in the log church, and having finished his visit, took an effectionate leave, and proceeded on his journey to Cincinnati, and thence to Warren county, where he owned a section of land adjoining what is now the town of Lebanon, [Ohio]. Eight years afterwards when I went to Phil[a] to attend lectures, I visited Jersey, and lodged a part of my time at his house. Two years afterwards, he started with his son and six daughters for a residence at Lebanon, but died in Pittsburg. You probably know some of his **descendents**.

I remember the visit of a very different personage—an itinerant *Tinker,* who, by the way, was a very useful man in those "early times." He was a small, middle aged man, who rode a **poney** and had under him a huge pair of coarse saddle bags, in which he carried his moulds, soldering irons, and every implement required in his vocation. He soldered up holes in our tin cups, turned old pewter basins into new, & did so many "choirs" in the line of his profession, that we were quite "made up." He was in all respects a queer character, but I was too young to analyse it. I mostly remember that father and mother were ready to laugh all the evening at his oddities, which, as it now seems to me, included bashfulness and affection. At the breakfast table next morning, when he had finished, he leaned back at an angle of 45°, and while in that posture, as I was passing, I happened to touch his chair and over he went, throwing his feet as high as the table. Father and mother could not restrain their laughter, tho' they attempted to scold me for being so careless. He scrambled up with his face as red as a gum leaf in October, and soon put off, having tinkered us up and afforded us new matter for conversation. You may think it strange that I relate this incident, but you should not; for the very fact of my remembering it 53 or 4 years shows the deep impression which it made on me. He presented a new aspect of character, and I saw the wonderful art of stopping up cracks in tin vessels with solder, and of casting pewter plates & basins. It was knowledge gained & monotony broken up—an impulse on the path of life. It was to me what (perhaps more than what) a far greater event would be to Frank, or Charlie, or Joe. We are not moulded at one operation, as our little Tinker made a quart basin, but hammered out by successive blows, & this was one of them. Happy is that child to whom the hammer is applied with skill! Happy may you and all the other parents to whom I write, count yourselves, if you can so direct it upon the little immortals whom God has committed to your tinkering, that when you are old their hearts will prompt them to rise up and call you blessed! ('Tis near 1 o'c'k — Adieu.)

Thursday, near 3 P.M. I might multiply my recollections of characters & events connected with society, which exerted on me an influence, good or bad, but have resolved to forbear, as my letter has already reached an appalling length. I might also trace out the history and fate or present condition, of several of my play mates & corn field companions; but, for the same reason, shall not. Indeed, a letter of 60 pages ought, I think, to be regarded under the law, as carried to the Maximum; and therefore, I subscribe myself your loving

Pa

THE REMINISCENTIAL PEN

THE SETTING

The preceding eight letters, written during a period of less than five weeks, are remarkable from many different angles. To have been written hurriedly, without premeditation or plan, they present an astonishing degree of integration as well as detail. Apparently with little effort Dr. Drake was able to relive his childhood and, from his "mind's eye," graphically portray its scenes. It is a thrilling feature to note that when the picture is not clear, he so states, and makes no effort whatever to fabricate. Therefore, we can accept all that he writes with implicit confidence that he is attempting to tell the absolute truth.

Letter Nine

THE REMINISCENTIAL PEN

Louisville, [Kentucky]
Thursday 3 P.M.
Jany 20th 1848.

My Dear Children of all classes:

I have just finished a letter of 64 pages, as, in fact, you know by having read it as a preliminary to this. It is (as you may recollect under this prompting) the 7th [eighth] which I have sent you, within a month, amounting to 240 or 50 pages. In these pages, written without premeditation or plan, and only 4 of them copied (to get rid of an error of logic in some of my *philosophical* reflections) I have embodied, in a truly off hand style the principal matters connected with the first 15 years of my [life] which seemed to me to have exerted much influence on my character and destiny. As you all know, a great change in my condition, position, and pursuits took place at that time; the history of which I gave in a letter to Dove two years ago; which letter, should *your* children ever have the curiosity to read what I have written, should be taken up after the rest—after the general epistle on which I am now engaged.[1]

---

[1] In accordance with this request, the letter written on December 20, 1845, which details the final preparations for the study of medicine has been placed last.

Charles has, by letter, proposed to me to continue my narrative on to the year 1820. If I were out of literary occupation, I might do so; but *as it is,* I must resist the temptation; and until I **git** out the 1ˢᵗ volume, at least, of my Physical and Medical History of our Great Valley, must lay aside the reminiscential pen. The letters I have written in a month have, of course, suspended writing on my book; but before I began them, I was not doing a great deal in that way; for I found it exceedingly difficult to write daily on one medical subject and lecture on another. But the writing down of reminiscences did not constitute any drawback on my lectures. On the contrary (myself being the judge) I have never lectured as well before; the *theory* of which I have already given in one of my epistles.

When I began my letter to Echo, I intended that it should be the last, and supposed it would reach about 30 pages. When I reached there, I thought what would follow would be too little for another, & so kept on. Could I have anticipated an extension to 60, I should have thrown it in two; & really hope you will not (have not) attempted to travel through it at a single reading.

I can not close without saying to you that I have written what I have written with a right good will; for *some* men love to write about themselves. Then it was pleasant to fall back upon and mingle once more with the family, and commune with father and mother, & play with the little children, & hear the babies cry. It was also pleasant to renew the friendships and pastimes and field emulations of boyhood. Finally, it was *delightful* to wander once more in the woods, and to sit down under the patriarchs of the forest, defended by their protecting arms from the heat of the summer sun, and listen to the songs of little birds above, or the voices of little insects in the flowers below, or to throw my hat over some luckless butterfly which happened to pass along.

In all the latter years of my life I have observed, that whenever I am intently reading or writing on *any subject whatever,* I am in some locality with which I was familiar in boyhood. When in reading Neal's History of the Puritans, I came to the Civil Wars & the Era of Cromwell, I had a map of London, Oxford, & other localities, drawn on a spot about half way between Mays Lick and Uncle Abraham's Upper Lee's Creek-mill, Certain large trees indicating the sites of the places named in the history. I had a locality in the same quarter for the prison in which John Bunyan was confined, and another for the stake at which John Rogers was burnt. And, what is remarkable, as often as I took up the work, the scenes were referred to the same spot, which is still, after several years, associated with them in my memory. In like manner, when writing on the laws of our climate, or combining the facts which establish the proper treatment of our Autumnal fever, I am in some one of these early sylvan scenes. As long as I continue to resume the same investigation, the same objects, unbidden, appear around me. I have never been able to discover anything in the subject which places me in the particular spot on which I find myself, nor do I know how far what I have said is true of others. In the letters which I have now brought to a close I was writing *of* those localities and their objects, all of which were *legitimately* before me, and

I was *there,* not *else*where in *imagination.* Thus, in narrating an event or a labour of any kind, the locality on which it was really performed was the one which was present to my mind. With such an *unconscious yearning,* to speak in paradox, towards the places dear to my boyhood, I could not fail to find great enjoyment in a *bona fide* imaginary review of them. In fact, after I got fairly started I was carried away by them, and couldn't stop if I would, till the subject was exhausted.

Should I ever resume my narrative, whatever interest you may take in it, mine will be much less. I have travelled through the romantic period, and feel sorry that I *have.* It is no longer in my contemplation as a pleasing task to be performed. I am like the child that has eaten up its sugar plum, after having for days enjoyed the anticipation of the feast. You are, as yet, too near the era of your childhood to be able to comprehend these feelings, but I hope you may all live to realize them. Yet I can not hope that such of you as have had the *misfortune* to pass your childhood & youth in the city, will ever find in your reminiscences the enjoyment which I have found.

That Heaven will bless and prosper & save you all, is the prayer of your affectionate

Father

BECOMING A DOCTOR

THE SETTING

Daniel Drake clearly recognized his totally inadequate preparation for the study of medicine. Yet, in spite of this handicap, his indomitable will and indefatigable industry associated with a brilliant mind enabled him to overcome all obstacles.

Letter Ten

BECOMING A DOCTOR

To Mrs. Alexander Hamilton McGuffey[1]

> Hybernaculum[2]
> Decr 20th, 1845
> Saturday night, 11 o'c'k.

My Dear Bettie—

I have just thrown upon the pile my 156th Sibylline leaf on Autumnal Fever, thus closing my "week's work."[3] Although my arm (your parti-coloured *robe de chambre* to the contrary notwithstanding) feels weary, and my fingers are a little cramped, I have begun, as you see, a new leaf on a new topic. When I shall finish it I can not tell; and when it will reach you I can not, Sibyl as I am, even prophesy, for my thermometer has been at cypher for two mornings, and is now only 4° above. Thus, not only are the river mails entirely suspended, but my cherished project of eating Christmas dinner with you is at an end. I can not

---

[1] Older daughter of Dr. Drake, Mrs. Alexander Hamilton McGuffey.

[2] The *hybernaculum*, according to Dr. Drake's beloved Linnaeus, was the winter cradle or protective covering of buds and bulbs. During the years covered by these letters Dr. Drake spent the period from about the first of November through the first week of March in Louisville, Ky.

[3] At this time Dr. Drake was engaged in writing the first volume of his monumental work to which reference has been made previously. See Letter II, Note 4, page 28.

even hope that this sheet will represent me on that festive occasion. Yesterday, I dispatched one to Sister B. [elle] but the boat returned after an ineffectual attempt to ascend the river, and my epistle is, I suppose, resting composedly in the L.P.O. If the obstructions were only to the upward voyage, I could bear it better; but when I think how many days may drag along before I receive a *bulletin de santé* from Dove-cote,[4] I feel rather fidgety. (Webster notes this word as *vulgar,* but I hope you will not take offense.)

As my letter to Sister B. was written on the anniversary of my arrival in C., so this is begun (perhaps will be finished) on the anniversary of the commencement of my medical studies. Since that time 45 years have rolled away, nearly 17 more than you have lived in the world. Of course, the circumstances of my arrangements for...the new Career (I had to look in the dictionary for the spelling of the last word, which will show you that I have not yet over-come the defects of the education with which I engaged in the study of my profession)... now rise dimly before me . . . as do the objects of a place from which we have departed, when we stop, turn round, and look back upon them. And still, there was much in the plans, labours, and occurrences of that year, to impress its memories more deeply on my heart than those of any year before, or of any year since, except that in which I gained, and that in which I lost, your dear Mother.

The long talked of project — that of "making me a doctor" — had at length been finally settled in the affirmative. I was

---

4 Dr. Drake's name for the home of "Dove," Mrs. A. H. McGuffey.

to enter on the study in a few months with my cousin, Dr John Drake, whose education was then nearly completed, and whose genius was only equalled by his great moral purity. With this prospect before me, he was taken ill in July with typhus fever, and died in August. This was my first disappointment, and it was a real misfortune to me, for *he* would have been a *good* preceptor, and I could have studied at home, & thus saved father an expense which he was in no way prepared to meet. He courageously persevered, however, in his cherished purpose, and I had to submit; although (on his account) I would have preferred being bound to a trades man; and had actually selected a master, Mr Stout, of Lexington, a sadler, to whom some of my cornfield companions had already gone.

But my preparatory education was not yet completed. True, I had learned to spell the words in old Dilworth, and a good portion of those in "Noah Webster, J^r, Esqr" whose spelling book then seemed to me a greater marvel than does at this time his quarto dictionary now lying before me. (By the way, how little did I *then* even dream, that I should ever have a son in law who could make a spelling book).[5] But I must fall back upon A.D. 1800, & continue the catalogue of my accomplishments in literature. As a reader, I was equal to any in what I regarded as the highest perfection—a loud & tireless voice; which I am sure you would say still inheres with me, if you had been within a hundred yards of the Institute,[6] during my lecture this morning. In

---

[5] Alexander Hamilton McGuffey, see Letter III, Note 1, page 41.

[6] The Louisville Medical Institute which became the Medical Department of the University of Louisville, Ky., in 1846.

chirography I was *so so,* in geography obscure, and in history, 0. In arithmetic, [I had gone] as far as the double rule of 3, practice, tare & tret, interest, and even a fraction in decimals. My greatest acquirement — that of which I was rather proud — was some knowledge of Surveying, acquired from Love (I mean to name the Author as well as my taste), but which I have long since forgotten. Of grammar I knew nothing, and unfortunately there was no one within my reach who could teach it. Limited as were my attainments, they exceeded that of many boys around me who knew much less.

Still, as I was "going to be a doctor," it was decided that I must have another "quarter's schooling." Accordingly, father subscribed again to "Master Smith," who kept in a log school house, on the banks of the Shannon in the woods, just 2 miles West of where we lived. Thirty six years afterwards, I visited the spot, and found the "old hickory" under which we used to play, quietly as ever casting off now & then his "shell-bark," with a personal appearance exactly the same as he wore in my boyhood. So I began to resume (I resumed) my suspended school studies. But the corn had to be hoed, and "seeding" time required the wheat field to be harrowed after the sower, and the seed had to be covered with the hoe near the numerous stumps, and it was **indispensible** for me to labour with my hands as well as head. So I had to rise at the dawn of day, and work in the field till breakfast time, then eat & start with my dinner in my hand. As the distance was 2 miles, I had to use my feet as well as my head & hands, and generally ran most of the way; as I do now in going to Dr Bayless' to breakfast.[7] Indeed I have always had such a propensity for running, that it seems a marvel that I never ran away.

But what did I do when I reached the consecrated log cabin? Why, work among the hard words in Webster, especially certain *outre* tables of monosyllables, and certain other tables of "words alike in sound, but different in signification and spelling," write, cypher, and read in "Scott's Lessons." (And this reminds me, again, that I have reached, from such small beginnings, to the distinction of having a son in law, who has complied a Reader almost as large as Scott's.)[8]

Meanwhile, to return to my narrative, other arrangements were making for the life before me, such as knitting socks, making coarse India muslin Shirts instead of tow linen, providing a couple of cotton pocket hand kerchiefs, and purchasing a white roram hat (which to my great grief, was stolen in less than a month after I reached C.)

It was also necessary that father should make a visit to Dr Goforth before I should be taken down, as a bargain was to be concluded. But before this was undertaken, a serious calamity fell upon us. Either three or four, I forget which, of the children, Sister Lizzy, Sister Lydia, Sister Lavinia, and your Uncle B. [enjamin] were all, about the same time,

---

[7] George Wood Bayless, M. D. (1817-1873), whose home was approximately two and a half *long* squares from Dr. Drake's room. At sixty, to have regularly run this distance, Dr. Drake must have been in good physical condition. Dr. Bayless was Demonstrator of Anatomy in the Louisville Medical Institute.

[8] Alexander Hamilton McGuffey, see Letter III, Note 1, page 41.

taken down with ague & fever; a disease never known before or since at the place where we lived. Some of them, especially Sister Lydia, continued with the disease for several weeks. In the midst of it, father got kicked by a horse on the instep of one of his feet, which became greatly inflamed, and a small spot mortified. This, of course, terminated my "schooling." I well remember the cares, toils, and anxieties of dear mother and myself; for every thing within and without now devolved upon us.

At last, when father had got well enough to travel, as the autumn was passing away, he determined to make his visit to the Doctor. He was gone about a week, and suffered a good deal in his foot from its hanging down. When he got back, he announced that all was arranged, and that I was to go down before the setting in of winter. I was to live in the Doctor's family, and he was to pay $400, provided I remained, as it was expected I would, four years, by which time, I was to be transmuted into a doctor, as I should then be 19! My whole time, however, was not to be given up to the study of medicine; for the D^r was to send me to School for two quarters, that I might learn Latin. But as was sagely decided, it was not to be done *before* I began the study of medicine, but at some future time.

My destiny now began to be a neighbourhood talk, and indeed, excited a considerable sensation. It was decided that I was to be a gentleman, and lead a life of ease and gentility. I was already called Doctor by some, and no one of the neighbours, old or young, passed me without having something to say about it. Some of them cautioned me against getting proud, & others, especially my good &

venarable old Uncle Cornelius, exhorted me to beware of bad young men and evil companions, of which he had understood there were a great many about Fort Washington, or "Cin." as it was sometimes called. Not a few of my young comrades were envious of me, and not a few of their mothers were in a similar plight in reference to mine — who showed such a proud disposition in wishing to make a "doctor of her son Dannel."

As to myself, I well recollect that this period of preparation at home, and critical agitation abroad, was by no means very joyous. I was fond of study, but not passionately so, and if I had any aspirations, they were not intense, and several circumstances conspired to countervail them. 1st I had looked into the medical books of my cousin, and found them so learned, technical, & obscure, that I was convinced my education was too limited. 2^{d} My father was too poor to pay for what he had undertaken, and was too ailing to dispense with my labours on the farm, now that I had got old enough to do half a man's work. 3^{d} I was a great homebody; had never been out of the family more than a day or a night "at a time"; felt timid about going among strangers in a town, and mingling with the "quality." Finally, I was distressed at the idea of an absence of 4 or 5 months. At length, all arrangements were made, and the 16th of Decr was fixed for my departure. Instead of starting on the journey I will start to bed, as I find it is after one o'c'k — *So good night, or, rather, morning.*

9 *A.M.* Having overslept myself, I did not run to Dr. Bayless' to breakfast this morning. After having done up

my work, I sat down to some excellent black tea, crackers, and dried beef, from which I have just risen. How many miserable and destitute people, old and young, there may now be (within sight of the dome of the Edifice in which I write) who are cold and hungry, I can not pretend to guess. What a delightful world this would be, notwithstanding its clouds and frosts, if every body around one was happy! It is in vain, however, to dream of such a condition, for human nature is so perverse that, as you have just seen, I was made unhappy at or by the thought that I was about going to Cin. to learn to be a Doctor and a gentleman! And this illustration reminds me of what I was about to tell you, when I threw down my pen 8 hours ago. When I was 15, travelling (spelled with 2 l's & I retain the habit, never losing an old attachment) — getting from one part of the country to another, I say, was a very different affair from what it now is (except when the river is frozen over), for one may now breakfast in Mayslick and sup in Broadway. In the first place, the roads were most of the way only "bridle paths," and even difficult to follow, for at their ramifications or "forks" there were no finger-boards, and not many living fingers to point the true way to the puzzled traveller. In the second place, between Mayslick and Cin., there were no taverns. Third, and lastly, as the said *via nova, deserta, obscura* was, also, *montosa et rugossissima,* the travel along it was slow and wearisome.

It results (or resulted) from these premises, that we had to provide some other means than the "cut money," which then made our small change. Accordingly mother put up a quantity of provisions, of which, at this late period, I recollect nothing but a couple of roast chickens and some bread. But before this stage of our preparations arrived, Father had been looking out for a travelling companion, as a winter journey back through such a wilderness, after parting from his "dear son Dannel," seemed to require the cheering companionship of a fellow traveller. At length he found one, a Mr Johnson (I think his name was Abram), who wished to see something of the country, and concluded to be of our party.

The morning of the 16 of Dec^r [1800] at length arrived, and the parting came with it. Lizzy was 13, Lydia 10, Benjn 6, Lavinia 3 or 4, & Livingston about one. There we all were in the cabin where more than half had been born, where I had carried the younger ones in my arms, and amused them with the good old cow brindle, as she drank her slop at the door while mother milked her. There too was "old lion," my friend and field and woods companion, in the midst of us, quite conscious that a journey was at hand, and by no means an uninterested member of the family. The parting over, we mounted, and he escorted us down the lane, which soon reached the woods & I took a farewell look at the little cabin, then wiped my eyes (for like dear Charlie's, "the water *would* keep coming into them"—crying, you see, runs in the blood) and set my face fairly to the West; and to the West, as you know, it has remained set for the 45 years that have since, by the Western rounds of the sun, been rolled away.

Our first 2 miles brought me in sight of the old hickory and its log school house on the banks of the Shannon. Our first halt, at noon, was in a village of a dozen cabins and 2 or 3 frames, called Germantown, where we stopped to feed, and dine at Dr Donaphan's. The D^r was an acquaintance of father's, and appeared to take an interest in me. He had studied awhile in Washington with Dr Goforth, before the D^r removed from there to Cin., and had been well acquainted with my Cousin, John Drake. He was a Virginian, a widower with one little daughter, a large man, was full of humour and scotch snuff, talked through his nose when it was not too full, and indulged in frequent and fluent fits of loud laughter.

After dinner we put off, and passing in the next 14 miles a few solitary cabins, by night reached Leathers' cabin and ferry, on the banks of the river [Ohio] opposite the mouth of Bull-Skin creek. Notwithstanding the unsavoury character of the locality, I must leave you for a while.

Mrs Gross' Parlour ½ past 2 P.M. With all the clothes I could put on including socks over my boots, I was so cold in Church this morning that I had to go near one of the stoves at the beginning of the Sermon. My eating no butter, and very little fat meat or indeed lean, diminished my heat generating (calorific) function. By instinct, as it were, I took a small size of pickled pork at dinner today, and expect thereby to be in a very stupid pickle in the course of half an hour. Mean while, I must hasten to relieve you from the unpleasant pickle in which I left you.

Mr Leathers' pennsylvania dutch Hotel consisted of a log cabin of one room, which was made to answer for bar, dormitory, refectory, and family apartments. The night, however, was not as cold as that we have just passed through, & as the blood of 15 is warmer than that of 60, I got on pretty well.

In the hope of reaching C.[incinnati] the next day, we made an early start. The river was about as high as it is now, and abounded in cakes of floating ice. I had not been on it before since I could remember, and had not yet learned to swim. Our ferry boat was of a small size, and my fears were very large. Our crew consisted of the old man & his daughter, a good looking, rosy faced damsel of 16 or 17. They toiled and twisted and dodged. My confidence increased as the voyage continued. We approached the shore of Ohio, and I (greatly delighted) escaped from the perils of the deep, realizing for the first time (for any thing I could then foresee) the truth of the maxim that he who is born to be &c, &c.

We mounted, and not only left the water, but the valley in which it flows. Our first halt was at Bohannon's, which was about 12 or 14 miles. There we dined & fed. We had not passed a house on the way. At the mouth of Big Indian, where point pleasant now is, we again descended to the river. Next, we halted and refreshed at Johns' mill on 15 mile creek...

Then we came to the mouth of the little Miami, and had to travel up it a mile, before we could ford it. There I was struck with the appearance of the trees which grow in the bottom lands, liable to frequent inundation. I had not before seen such a locality. A mile further brought us into the then village of Columbia, and also brought twilight. By this time it was beginning to rain & had been thawing all day. In the center of the place there was a tavern, kept in a two story log house, and we "put up" for the night. Father and myself lodged in one bed, and Mr Johnson in the other. In the course of the night the cords hurt him through the feathers, which were then a scarce article, and the cord (quite as scarce an article) broke in one place; where upon he took his knife, and cutting round, let himself down on the floor.

At day light next morning we were off, intending to breakfast at Dr Goforth's. It rained, and the mud had become deep. Between the lower end of Col.[umbia] and the upper end of Cin.[cinnati] (below Deer Creek bridge), there were two cabins—one half way, the other where Kilgour's garden comes to the street on the river bank. We passed the post office, then kept by Mrs Oliver's father in front of Mr Symmes', and made our way to Peach Grove, where Mrs Lytle now lives; the grounds through which we reached it being, near the house, embellished with corn stalks, from which the ears had been lately pulled. Father remained a day, when, to my dismay, he took leave of me, and I took to **Chesselden's** Anatomy.[9]

My health is good. The Bayless, Gross & Shorts are well, except Sally who has a pain in her face. The affairs of our Institute are still in a morbid condition.

I am greatly disturbed at the thought that Harriet may not have reached you, during the open weather. Her last letter to me was dated on the fourth inst.

---

[9] William Cheselden (1688-1752), English surgeon and author of the most widely used *Anatomy of the Human Body* in the eighteenth century. In England, thirteen editions of this book appeared between 1713 and 1792. There were also several American editions in addition to a German translation.

I wish you all "both great & small"—a merry Christmas. Perhaps the river may permit me *in person,* to wish you a happy New Year.

With two handfuls of love to Dear Charlie, and *quantum sufficit* to all the rest, including Aunt Lydia and Caroline, when you may see them, and also Cousin Sue & her better half, and the Campbells and Grahams, I remain as ever

Your most affectionate

Father

INDEX

INDEX

Bunyan, John, 195
Butler, Bishop, 117
Byron, Lord, 76n

Cabin, pioneer's, 15, 24
Cahills, 179
Caldwell, Charles, 51n; Mrs. Charles, 157
California, 107
Campbell, James Parker, 73; Mrs. J. P. (Harriet Echo Drake), 3, 23, 24, 41, 118, 175
Campbell, Graham & Co., 183
Canada, xxiv
Cartwright, Samuel A., 193, 203, 204n, 210, 212, 222
Casey, Mrs. 223
Cemetery, Spring Grove (Cincinnati, Ohio), xxvii
Centre College, 91n
Charcoal, 86
Charles II of England, 57n
Chartier's Creek, 214, 215, 216
Chattanooga Public Library, x
Cheese making, 98
Cherokee Indians, 7n
Cheselden, William, xii, 246n
Chesterfield, Lord, 165
Chickasaw Indians, 7n
Chillicothe, Ohio, 73, 209
Chinn, Mrs., 28
Chippewa Indians, 58
Cincinnati, Ohio, xiii, xiv, xvi, xxvii, 12, 22, 30, 37n, 43, 45, 69, 96, 105, 142, 159, 176, 187, 194n, 195, 198, 208, 209, 241, 242, 244, 245, 246
Cincinnati College, xviii, xxiii; General Hospital, viii; Library Society, xviii; Public Library, x; Observatory, 121n; Society for the Promotion of Agriculture, xviii

Clark, Gen. George Rogers; Governor William, 92n
Clark, Master, 142
Clarke, Robert & Co., v
Clay, Henry, xxi, 208
Clergyman, vii
Cloth, dyeing of, 101
Collectivism, vi
Columbia, Ohio, 11, 245, 246
Congress, The Library of, x
Contents, xxxi
Conway, Judge, 207
Corn husking, 55; Indian, see maize; cornmeal, 57
Cornwallis, Lord, 61n
Corryell's Ferry, 9
Craig [surname], 193
Crawford, Col. William, 216, 219
Crerar Library, John, vii
Cresap [Capt. Michael], 216, 219
Cromwell, [Oliver], 231
Crusoe, Robinson, 167
Cumberland Mountains, 34n
Currency, of the Confederation, 85n; of Kentucky, 33n
Curry, Master Hiram Miram, 34, 36, 143

Darwin, Charles, 76n
Darwin, Erasmus, 75, 76n
Davies, Godfrey, xi
Day, Mrs.; Morgan; Katy, 82
Delaware Indians, 216; River, 9
Deer Creek, 246
Deer hunting, 217
Desha, Gen. Joseph; Gen. Robert, 156
Devil, "raising" and "laying," 216
Dickinson, [John], 165
Dilworth, Thomas, 146n; *Spelling Book*, 8, 146, 164, 237

INDEX

Doctor, Becoming a, 235

Donaphen, Dr., 244

Dove, see McGuffey, Mrs. Alexander H.

Drake, Abraham, 5, 13, 28, 34, 35, 59, 130, 157, 187, 231

Drake, Benjamin, 36, 194, 239, 243

Drake, Charles Daniel, v, 21, 41, 220n; Mrs. C. D., 91

Drake, Cornelius, 5, 13, 28, 151, 187, 192, 197, 207, 241

Drake, Daniel, activities in Cincinnati, Ohio, xiv, xviii; ancestry, 4; anniversaries, 22; biographical sketch, xiii; burn of, 37n; aids establishment of Commercial Hospital, xx; birth, 6; cabin home, 15; character, xxix; Cincinnati College established, xviii; collects information for treatise on the diseases of the Mississippi Valley, xxiv; cook on flatboat, 105; death, xxvii; *diploma,* xiv; Dr. Benjamin W. Dudley's accusations, xvi; earns first money, 33; educator, xvi; *Inaugural Discourse on Medical Education,* xix; editorials, xxv; method of erasure, [72]; establishes medical journal, xxii; evaluations of his "classic" *Treatise,* xxvi; expelled from The Medical College of Ohio, xx; faithfulness, 32; fathers The Medical College of Ohio, xvii, xix; *The Franklin of Cincinnati,* xxviii; friend of Henry Clay, xxi; history, concept of, vi; host to Cincinnati visitors, xviii; literary style, xxviii; marriage of, xv; *Mays Lick, Diseases of,* xv; memory, first, 15; names Ohio, 37n; *Notices Concerning Cincinnati,*

Drake, Daniel, *continued*
xv; opinion of Dr. Samuel D. Gross, xxvii; parades in Dr. Gross' parlor, 222; *Picture of Cincinnati,* xvi; playmates (early), 28; poem, 184; preparation for study of medicine, 241; *Principal Diseases of the Interior Valley of North America . . . ,* xxvi; professorships in Lexington, Ky., xvi, xxi; in Cincinnati, xix, xxiii, xxvii; in Philadelphia, xxiii; in Louisville, xxiv, xxvii; public lectures on botany, xvii; punishment, 31; receives M.D. degree, xvi; scholarship, [40], [140]; school, first, 33; schoolmates, 156; sells whiskey, 85; *Slavery, Letters on,* vii; spelling by, viii; student at University of Pennsylvania, xiv, xvi; style as a lecturer, xxiii, xxiv; suggests school for blind, xxv; traits, early, 6; tribute to mother, 111

Drake, Elizabeth, 8, 16, 26, 59, 65, 95, 104, 108, 109, 122, 224, 239, 243

Drake, Elizabeth Mansfield, (Dove,) 141n; see McGuffey, Mrs. A. H.

Drake, Sir Francis, 164

Drake, Harriet Echo, 3n; see Campbell, Mrs. James P.

Drake, Harriet Sisson, xv, xxvii

Drake, Isaac, 5, 13; arrives at Limestone, Ky., 10; books owned by, 8, 161, 162; first home in Kentucky, 11; purchases farm, 14; second farm, 36; suit against, 32; shortcomings of, 113

Drake, Jacob, 53, 159, 207

Drake, Dr. John, 157, 159, 162, 203, 221, 236, 244

INDEX